Philip Reed is one of the world's leading professional modelmakers, and he has built models for clients in both North America and Europe. His work has also included restoration projects for leading galleries and museums.

BUILDING A MINIATURE NAVY BOARD MODEL

PHILIP REED

Foreword by Michael Wall

Seaforth
PUBLISHING

Copyright © Philip Reed 2009

This edition first published in Great Britain in 2013 by
Seaforth Publishing,
Pen & Sword Books Ltd,
47 Church Street,
Barnsley S70 2AS

www.seaforthpublishing.com

British Library Cataloguing in Publication Data
A catalogue record for this book is available from the British Library

ISBN 978 1 84832 186 1

Typeset and designed by Mousemat Design
Printed in Singapore through MRM Graphics Ltd

ᴄᴏ *Contents* ᴏᴄ

⨳ *Foreword* ⨳

In this, his third, book, *Building a Minature Navy Board Model*, Philip Reed carefully takes the reader through the process of his approach to the minature replication of a late seventeenth-century Navy Board ship model. His 1/16in = 1ft (1:192) scale model of *Royal George* not only exemplifies the traditional skill of past artisans but, in my professional opinion, raises the bar by crafting a detailed model at one-quarter of the normal scale (1:48 or 1/4in = 1ft. Mr Reed's finished extreme miniature model of the British three-decker *Royal George* is an astonishing work and will no doubt inspire present and future modellers to emulate his methods. Without question, this model not only perpetuates his international celebrity in this genre, but now places him in a realm of his own.

Among avid modellers there is a widely held consensus that the construction of a replica Navy Board style ship model is one of the most difficult endeavours that a modeller can undertake. I often call them the 'ship modeller's model'. The structural elements of such period ship design are complex, and to successfully produce the required exposed framing, full interior arrangements, metal smiting of armament and fittings, and the usual extensive carving and painted decorative elements appears a daunting task. However, in this book, the author offers a detailed photographic sequence and a well written text that provides the reader with his step-by-step method. There is no other book that so superbly covers the unique construction progression in a clear, complete, and unpretentious manner.

In this day of the overwhelming popularity of contemporary and modern art, often produced very quickly and with materials that will not stand the test of time, it is a joy to know that someone so artistically talented has committed himself to such a traditional art form and is willing to openly share his knowledge and techniques with his fellow modellers.

I have had the honour to represent Philip Reed and his extraordinary work for the past twenty years and can personally attest to his utmost diligence in investigating and obtaining only the most authentic information about his model subjects. *Building a Miniature Navy Board Model* is a must-have for either the amateur or professional ship builder's library.

Michael Wall
Director of the American Marine Model Gallery

❧ *Introduction* ❧

A childhood visit to the National Maritime Museum at Greenwich was my first introduction to the world of ship models, and it had a profound effect on me. The models that so imprinted themselves on my memory were the Navy Board models of the seventeenth and eighteenth centuries. I have such clear memories of the complexity of the exposed frames and the brass cannons peering through their ports, probably because of my child's view, looking up at most of them, and having only occasional views of the decks when lifted up. So the model of *Royal George*, which forms the core of this book, marks for me something of coming full circle, of finally building a three decker, a project that was put on hold until my semi-retirement from professional modelmaking when I would have the time to devote to such an absorbing task. It is, however, probable that I would never have embarked on the building of miniature Navy Board models had it not been for the inspiration received from the books and work of Donald McNarry. His models in general had a huge influence on me but it was particularly his miniature Navy Board work that had the greatest impact and his support when building some of my early efforts was invaluable. The method I used for the framing on *Royal George* was pioneered by him, and this framing technique is described by him in various issues of the British journal *Model Shipwright*.

Navy Board Models

What are Navy Board models and what are their distinctive characteristics? At the simplest level, the archetypal examples are those part-planked, framed ship models of naval vessels, built approximately in the hundred years after 1650, which have their frames exposed below the wale and have, as their crowning glory, the most detailed and beautifully crafted decoration. Few were rigged. There is, however, much more to them than this, and though our knowledge of their purpose and their creators is hazy, there are significant characteristics that set them aside from other types of ship model and make them highly collectable and an attractive proposition for the modern ship modeller.

'Navy Board' is not the only term by which they are known. They are often described as 'Dockyard' or 'Admiralty' models and these different names give us some clues about them. Dockyard suggests their provenance and perhaps hints at their purpose, while the terms Navy Board and Admiralty allude to their recipients, for it is our understanding that many were commissioned by these boards. Today, Navy Board is the commonly used term and is the one we shall use throughout the book.

Though we can define them simply, we need also to be aware of how they differed, and of how they developed over the hundred years. Their scale is generally 1:48, a quarter inch to the foot, which is usually the same scale as was used for ships' draughts and this has led some commentators to conclude that there is some link between the two, that they fulfilled the function of the ship plan; this seems unlikely, however. Some were not built to this scale, and the amount of detail, along with the repetition of component parts, would have been unwarranted for the needs of a shipwright. Furthermore, though the overall models were built to a scale, the framing was not, and is distinctly stylised. It does not ape the framing patterns of the prototypes but follows a simpler system. Though there were variations, the hull frame of a Navy Board model consists generally of three parts: the floor timber, futtock and top timber. It is conceivable that this pattern was not that different to the full-sized framing of early seventeenth-century vessels. By the beginning of the eighteenth century, however, ships had grown considerably and the greater size required heavier framing and scantlings and multiple floor timbers, futtocks and top timbers. This development is partly reflected in Navy Board models for certainly in the later models the framing is built, if not identically, then closer to the prototypes. The thickness of the frames and the adjacent spaces, however, known as the 'timber and room' and later as the 'room and space', were built to scale and reflected the dimensions that were specified for particular Rates.

This open framing adds so much to the beauty of the Navy Board model; light and shadow play across the frames while the delicate skeletal structure is subtly defined by light shining though the hull; in the dark recesses there is mysterious space. And all this, of course, is made possible by the absence of planking below the lower wale. Above this the hull was planked with either individual planks or a sheet of timber or veneer up to the upper wale. Decks are generally left only partially planked with strips of planking fitted along the centerline and at the sides. This was usually cut from a single strip of timber and was frequently scored to

The engraving of the *Royal George* (© National Maritime Museum, Greenwich, London).

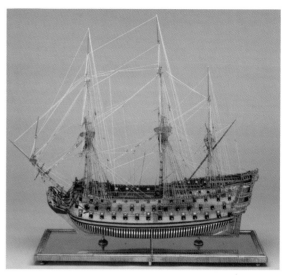

ABOVE: The rigged model of *Royal William* (©
National Maritime Museum, Greenwich, London).

LEFT: The quarter galleries of the unrigged model
of *Royal William* (© National Maritime Museum,
Greenwich, London).

represent the individual planks. Grating is often
fitted, and this further compounds the
suspicion that the modellers were seeking to
create an intricate, jewel-like beauty that had a
meaning beyond the simple shape and structure
of the ship.

If we get a sense of this looking at the
frames and planking, our breath is taken away
by the details and decoration found on many.
Gun port lids, often open and revealing
cannon, are fitted with finely modelled hinges
and surmounted with beautifully carved rigols.
Capstans and stairways are shown, channels and
deadeyes fitted, and rudders with braces of brass,
fastened with tiny rivets, are hung on miniature
gudgeons. Fibre optics and modern photographic techniques have revealed remarkable detail
deep within the hull of some models, details that
the original creator must have assumed would be
hidden forever. And the crowning glory to all
this is the carving: the carving of the stern and
quarter galleries, the entry port and figure-

head. Mythological figures mingle with the
most finely carved and gilded decoration, which
is beautifully set off by the richness of the
natural wood. Paintwork is sparingly used on
the insides of gun port lids and on wales, and on
bulkheads and rails.

What was the function of these rich and
exquisite objects, these beautiful examples of
miniature craftsmanship? We have discounted
their usefulness as plans and so it seems unlikely
that they were submitted as designs. Some
models are later than the ships they represent
and by the beginning of the eighteenth century,
simple block models were being used for design
purposes. So their purpose is really quite a
mystery. One suggestion is that they were built
at the same time as the prototype, in tandem
with the full-scale version, to help visualise what
the ship might look like, and the absence of
planking certainly helps to understand the
underwater shape of the ship more clearly. The
fact that some models have gun ports which

have been closed up and positions for masts which have been moved, suggests that changes were being made during the building of the full-size ship which were reflected in the models. The internal arrangements, so difficult to see in the finished model, may have been constructed to help in the layout down below and would, of course, have been clearly visible as the model was being built and discussed.

It is known that some were built as commissions and made in a private capacity for individuals; the Fourth Rate *Centurion* was made for Lord Anson in the 1740s. Pepys, in his diary, certainly covets a model and he built up a collection that, unlike his library, was at some stage dispersed. The pleasure of a thing in miniature is something that all ship modellers recognise; the admirals and administrators of the Navy three hundred years ago seemingly felt the same. These were simply beautiful records of what ships looked like; they were like a painting, but a three-dimensional portrayal.

Yet another theory is that they were a form of advertising and were presented as gifts to the Admiralty Board from dockyards soliciting work, their quality reflecting what the Board might expect in the full-size version.

Though we know little about the builders of all these models it is certain that they were built by shipwrights. Some may have been made by young apprentice shipwrights as part of the process of learning the art of shipbuilding. There may have been other skilled craftsmen involved; certainly the quality of some of the miniature metal work, sometimes rendered in silver, suggests that jewellers may have been employed. While there is some difference in the quality of the work, throughout the period the standard of craftsmanship was consistently high and sets a high bar for those of us aiming to emulate those skills in the twenty-first century.

Royal George

My choice of subject stems from a chance encounter with one of the unrigged models of the First Rate *Royal William* of 1719 in the National Maritime Museum. When visiting on some quite different business I was so taken with the model that I decided there and then that I would build a model of either her or one of the other ships in her class as soon as I could find the time. The *Royal William* was launched in 1719 but was never fitted for sea as a 100-gun ship but was cut down to a Second Rate in 1756. She was finally hulked in 1790. There are no plans available of her because she was built to the dimensions of the *Royal Sovereign* of 1701, lines plans of which are held by the National Maritime Museum at Greenwich.

Over the following months, I accumulated odds and ends of information and a year or so later, made a special trip to the museum to photograph the model. This was made possible through the help afforded by the staff and because it was not at that time on display in one of the public galleries. I took plenty of photographs, close up and from all angles, and they proved invaluable, particularly when constructing the head and stern. However, it was soon after this, while pondering the expense and delay involved in obtaining a set of draughts from the National Maritime Museum, that I switched my choice of subject to *Royal George*. Like *Royal William*, she was cut down to a Second Rate of 90 guns in 1745, renamed *Royal Anne* in 1756 and was finally broken up in 1767. I already had a copy of a rather aged, but beautifully illustrated catalogue of ship models at the Museum of Fine Arts, Boston, that contained a broadside view and nine excellent close-ups of their model of *Royal George*, and a set of plans for her. The plans I had were prepared from the original draughts in the National Maritime Museum by Norman Swales. His drawings are accurate and impeccably researched, and readers may have come across his work in the recently published volumes of *British Warships in the Age of Sail* by Rif Winfield. The plans were, as would be expected at this early date, lines and profile only. It is rare for deck plans to be included at

The beautiful, rigged model of *Royal George* (Photograph © 2009 Museum of Fine Arts, Boston).

this time, and it was left to the shipwright to plot the disposition of hatches and other fittings around the position of the masts, so I had to prepare my own plans for the decks, which I deal with later in the book.

In terms of finishing it was *Royal William* that was the real inspiration for this project, in my opinion one of the finest models of its type for the period, exhibiting some exquisitely executed carving, all finished with plain varnish. The wale, upper works and some details are black, while the only colour is the dull red inside to hull and port lids. However, when I switched subjects to *Royal George* I had to think again. After much deliberation, I decided that my model would try to stay true to *Royal William* model in spirit and finish while following the plans and photographs I had of *Royal George*. In addition to these models, I had the contemporary engraving of *Royal George* (see page 8), a copy of which I found as endpapers in *The Ship of the Line, Volume 2* by Brian Lavery. Before starting work on the model, I spent a great deal of time perusing this profile along with some photographs I already had of the rigged model of *Royal William*. So I had a fair amount of information, certainly enough to build a model of a First Rate ship of this period, but as to building an accurate model of *Royal George*, that was more problematic. When researching any historical ship one has to be so careful with the material you unearth; there is so much inaccurate information out there that you must check everything and trust nothing. But a Navy Board model is somewhat different because the majority of these are simply identified by establishment and rate. Named vessels are comparatively few, and their identification is sometimes brought into question. When researching *Royal George*, I certainly found many startling differences and incongruities between the different models, the plan and the engraving. The differences are so many that apart from the basic structure of the hull, there are few timbers of the head or stern from one source that are even remotely similar to those from another, and the numbers and layout of deck beams are similarly and interestingly varied.

The Model

The model was built to my usual scale of 16ft to 1in, 1:192, which is a quarter of the size of the original Navy Board models. The actual building follows fairly tried and tested methods for framing and planking, and these are described in detail in the main part of the manual. One major innovation in the build is the two-part hull. I had not built a three-decker before and was somewhat concerned about the difficulty of fitting the fully framed decks from above. The tumblehome and narrow topsides, combined with the broad waterline, made the prospect of fitting beam shelves, carlings and ledges deep inside the model daunting indeed, so I decided to find a way of delaying the assembly of the two sections as long as possible. Initially, I planned to fit the lower gun deck before gluing together the upper and lower sections of the hull and then carry on working from above, reaching down inside the hull to do the work, as I had always done in the past, in order to complete the decks; but, in practice, I found I was able to fit both lower and middle decks to the lower framed section and all the upper decks to the upper section, before, very reluctantly, gluing the two sections of the model together. Not only did this make a lot of the work much more straightforward and more pleasant to execute but also it made it possible to easily and accurately position the beam shelves and establish the correct thickness of the ships side.

Although much of the intricate work involved in correctly framing the lower decks will be all but invisible from above it will still be seen through the open ports surprisingly well, particularly if the model is lit from above, as demonstrated in some of the photographs. This seemed an excellent reason for presenting this model unrigged and unarmed, with the port lids raised well out of the way to ensure maximum visibility, and Navy Board convention is more closely followed.

I hope the whole topic of Navy Board construction does not seem too daunting. I built my first Navy Board model many years ago and still remember the thrill it gave me as it gradually took shape, far more easily than I could have ever dreamt. If you have bought this book with the intention, however tenuous, of making a first attempt at this rather specialised style of modelmaking, then one of the smaller vessels from the period would seem the obvious choice. Although I have demonstrated the process here with a model of a large First Rate, the text and photographs could equally be used for the building of a vessel of any size from this period, and a smaller prototype would allow for the omission of a lot of the complex work involved in a large three-decker.

If you do choose a different ship, I would strongly recommend taking as your subject an existing model to which you can gain access and for which plans and photographs are available, and preferably one that you will be allowed to photograph – check your museum first. Also search for paintings or engravings of the ship; their accuracy may be questionable but the more reference, the better.

These models are not easy to build, at whatever scale you choose, but practice and patience will go a long way, and certainly there can be no better example to aspire to than a Navy Board model.

Photography

Though I once taught creative photography, now my camera is used as an aid to research and as a means of recording my own work. Four years ago, rather reluctantly, I switched to a digital camera that I used, hand held, with rather mixed results. I found it the ideal solution for putting together text and photographs, day to day, as the work on a model progressed. but my focus was on the work in hand rather than on learning new photographic skills, so the photos went to the printed page little changed from their original format. I then changed my camera for a digital SLR and this solved the problems I had with both focusing and depth of field. Using the new camera with a light and portable carbon fibre tripod, and with the camera set in the Av mode at f. 29 with a ten-second delayed exposure made a huge improvement in the quality of the photographs and gave me added flexibility when needing both hands in the picture. I have also brought to bear the facilities of Photoshop, which, though complex, have been a great asset. I have aimed to edit down the highlights and shadows to give the clearest visual description of the task depicted but I am forced to admit that although the pictures may gain in clarity they do sometimes lose some of their original ambience; I have done my best to do as little editing as possible to the photographs of the completed model that are to be found throughout the book. As with the building of models, so with photography, we learn as we go; each day, through trial and error, we learn a little more.

ᴄᴏ Navy Board Model Collections ᴄᴏ

T he list of major collections is not long. First, in terms of size and quality, comes the National Maritime Museum at Greenwich, with something in the region of 250 Navy Board models. The Naval Academy at Annapolis has the second largest collection, with some four dozen models, mainly English but also including one French, one Spanish, and one very old so-called Italian model, now mainly the hull only. The next largest collection is at the Science Museum with some thirty models. Then comes the privately owned Kriegstein Collection, numbering nineteen British models, one French, and one Dutch. The Thomson Collection, recently bequeathed to the Art Gallery of Ontario, Toronto, contains more than a dozen British dockyard models, plus more than fifty French POW models and all sorts of other treasures. There are five English Navy Board models in St Petersburg (some much maligned), five stunning examples at the Pitt-Rivers Museum at Oxford, four in the Hillhouse Collection in Bristol, a couple at Trinity House, London, a half dozen in Merseyside, Liverpool, and various and sundry models in private hands as well as smaller museums. (With thanks to Major Grant Walker, US Naval Academy Museum, Annapolis).

This fine model of *Royal William* depicts the First Rate as she was designed in 1714. It now resides in the collection of the US Naval Academy Museum at Annapolis. Note the conspicuous ivory blocks.

Building
Royal George 1715

∽ *The Hull Frames* ∾

This part describes the building of the framed part of the hull up to and including the lower gun deck, and it is this stylised framing that really defines the Navy Board model. Above the lower gun deck the model is carved out of the solid.

The first task is to prepare templates. I had made a number of copies of the body-plan, taken from the Norman Swales plans, and these were mounted on 10 thou plastic card with double-sided tape from which I then cut the templates to be used for the framing. I had also prepared some timber for the framing of the model – Brazilian boxwood. It is easier to work than many other boxwoods and has a light buff colour, less yellow and dense than many others. However, there are other options, but timber for this sort of work needs to be close-grained and fairly hard. Sycamore, holly or beech are suitable alternatives; other modellers use lime or basswood, but I find it too soft and woolly for this purpose.

The next job is to ascertain the thickness and then the number of frames and spaces along the length of the model, and there is really only one accurate and realistic way to achieve this. First, you will need a copy of the plans and a photograph of a Navy Board model of the ship of which you are building a miniature, or one of a similar vessel. Now mark on the plans profile where the foremost and aftermost full frames will be positioned by carefully referring to the photograph, then count the number of frames and spaces on the photograph of the model between these two points; the total will be the number of frame sections required for this part of the model. From now on it is a matter of trial and error. You will take the boards from which you intend making the sections and pass them through the sander until you think you are reaching the correct thickness; it is the time to remove a small piece from the end of one of these, cut it into a number of pieces, place these together and take an accurate measurement of their combined thickness. If, for instance, you have put eight pieces together, the overall measurement will be equal to four frames and four spaces. Now set a pair of dividers to this measurement and work along the length of the plan between the two lines to see how many frames and spaces you would achieve using this thickness of timber. If there are too few, they will need more sanding; if, however, there are too many, then I am afraid you have to start again. This is what we mean by trial and error.

Timber

The standard width of the box I had was 3in (as available from my particular supplier), just too narrow for the midship breadth of *Royal George*. Rather than cut the sections lengthways from the 3in strip (so wasting an awful lot of the precious timber) I decided to try a slightly different technique for the wide midship frames. It worked quite successfully, and the remaining and narrower fore and aft frames were all dealt with in the orthodox way as will become clear shortly. Incidentally, this problem is only likely to occur when building a First Rate at this scale; a 74-gun ship fits comfortably onto a 3in board with very little waste.

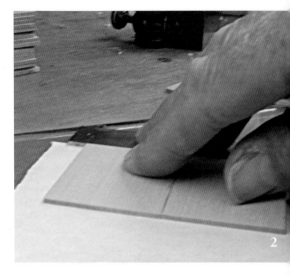

1.

Timber for the midship frames, or sections as we will describe them, is being prepared. The 3in-wide strip has been run down to just over half the breadth of the ship. The saw has been set up to cut rectangles of box that are the same height as the framed lower section of the ship.

2.

Two pieces, which will form a single section, are being superglued together on some non-stick backing paper. It is laid over a sheet of glass to ensure that the two pieces are absolutely level. They are being held in place with the far edges butting up against a small steel straightedge while the glue dries.

3.

Templates have been prepared and are here being used to mark out midship sections ready for cutting. The steel bar is just a useful reference to butt up both timber and template to. Only half the final number are required. All the templates shown here, and later in the book, are prepared from copies of the plans, and mounted with double-sided tape on 10 thou plastic card.

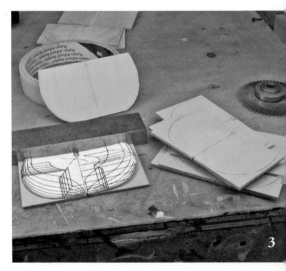

4.

After cutting to size, the sections are carefully slotted so that they can be located with precision on the building jig. I used a band saw with a narrow fine-toothed blade for this job but a hand-held fretsaw would do the job just as well.

5.

The template used for shaping the frame sections has been modified by being hollowed out. The remaining area of the template at the sides and base has to be sufficient to accommodate the final depth and length of the extra floor and top timbers which will be glued on to add strength to the section and represent another frame. The top edge has been trimmed to include the locating slot. The frames are marked out (front right), before the strips of box (top left) are used to cover the outer area of each of the sections.

6.

It is now time to glue up before fitting the strips which will represent the floors and futtocks. The three inner blobs of glue are Seccotine (which will later allow the sections to be prised apart) and the four outer blobs Superglue. The latter correspond with the overlaps between the top timbers, futtocks and floors.

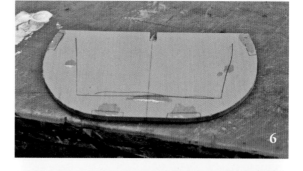

7.

The boxwood strips have been glued in place and tacked between suitably sized pieces of glass. A weight can then be placed on top of the stack while drying. When all the midship frames have been so treated they can be turned over and the surplus wood around the edges removed on the band saw.

8.

In the foreground are some of the trimmed frames so treated, some of which are being glued and clamped together on the building jig. In the background are the remaining single-piece sections, from fore and aft, which are narrow enough to fit crossways on the 3in strips of wood.

9.

In the previous photograph, some of the mid ship frames are shown glued and clamped. However, before this was done I used any off cuts from the original strips that I had, and there are always plenty of these, to act as spacers. They were glued in place with a few spots of Seccotine, and then the whole frame was treated with a few more spots, as can be seen on the frame in the left foreground, before adding it to those already clamped in the jig. Four or five can easily be glued up at one time.

10.

The work now continues along very straightforward lines, gluing each frame to the previous frame, just taking care that they are all pressed firmly down on the jig before clamping. Seccotine is not a hugely strong adhesive and it will allow you to prise apart the sectionss at a later stage.

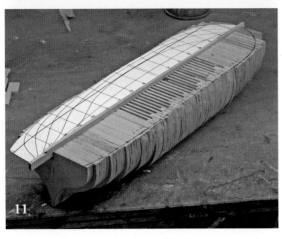

11.

A template from the lines plan is now prepared for the top of the frames and the outline marked in. Note the stern section has not yet been built up.

12.

Using a rough carbide cutter and drum sander, the model is now roughly shaped. This job can, of course, be done with a variety of hand tools such as rasps, but having a flexible shaft tool makes the job very much easier and a lot faster.

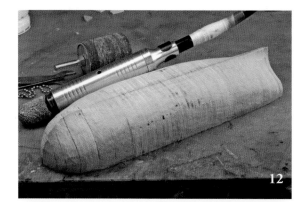

13.

Now we have to get to grips with the stern. If you examine the stern of a Navy Board model you will see that in most instances the aftermost complete frame, or fashion piece, is set at an angle, the two previous frames joining it part low down. This is what we now have to replicate. The first step is to make a card jig of the angle between the keel and the fashion piece and set the sander to it.

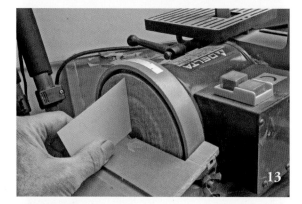

14.

Now the stern of the model is sanded to this angle.

15.

One of the edges of all the strips of box to be used for the transoms is sanded to the same angle, as are both ends of the block of box for the filling piece.

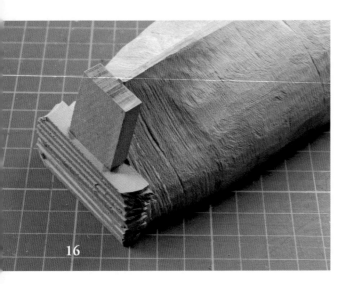

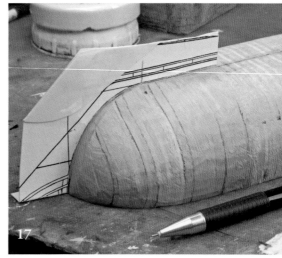

16.

These timbers are now assembled as shown here. A piece of suitable veneer is fitted between each of the transoms and the whole structure glued together with spots of Seccotine for easy dismantling.

17.

A series of templates can now be prepared for all sections, such as the waterlines, stern and bow, which is shown here.

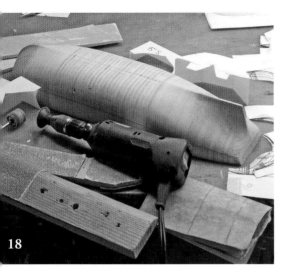

18

19

18.

Using drum and disk sanders in the Minicraft drill, and a selection of home-made sanding boards, the model is sanded to its final shape. Some of the templates that were used can be seen around the model. To the right are those for the various sections and to the left are those for the waterlines at bow and stern. These were made from plastic card and built up to the correct height with other strips.

Working with plastic card and Superglue is quick and easy, and it does ensure that the templates are offered to the hull at exactly the right level.

19.

A template has been made to mark in the lower edge of the wale. This will be an important reference point for the framing, because the top timbers will extend just below it, about 1/8in amidships and tapering off slightly fore and aft.

20.

Now a length of masking tape is fitted around the hull where the top timbers will end and a line is drawn along it with a fine ballpoint pen.

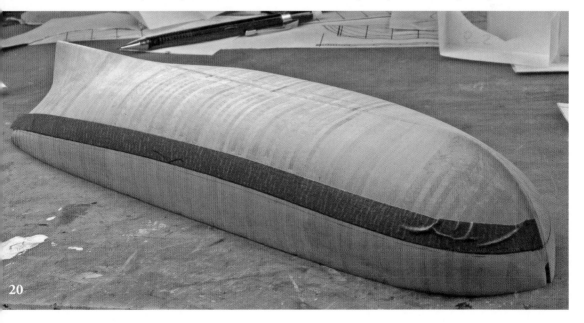

20

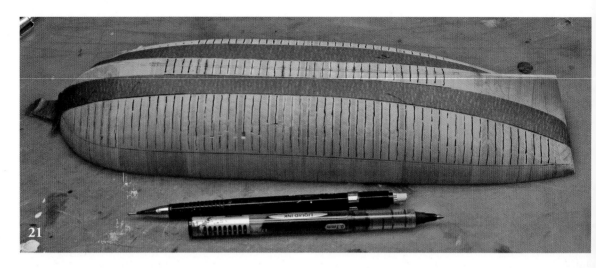

21.

The next job is to apply another strip of tape to cover the hull where floors and futtocks overlap. There appear to be no hard and fast rules for positioning this, the best guide being to replicate the run on the model you are using as a prototype, or at least choose as a guide a model of similar date and class. Ultimately, it is a matter of doing it by eye. When you are satisfied with the position and have checked that both port and starboard are identical, the two edges of both the tape are used once more to draw lines on the hull. Now all those alternate frames between the futtocks and floors that will be removed are marked, along their centres, with a ballpoint pen.

22.

The model has been turned over and the frames numbered. I have also ruled in a series of diagonal lines that will assist in the accurate and easy reassembly of the model later on.

23.

Using a sharp, fine-bladed knife the model is now prised apart. I divided it into units of four frames

amidships, where there is a minimal change of ship shape, and doubles as soon as the taper at fore and aft becomes more pronounced. Now a pair of compasses were adjusted so that the point extended about 1/8in further than the lead and the depth of the frame, was marked around the edge, the point, of course, resting against the edge of the blank. Frame depth has to be estimated and at this scale, if it looks right, it probably is about right. Floors will be deeper than futtocks and top timbers.

24.

Because the floors are deeper than the futtocks and top timbers, a second line is drawn in as a guide. All the marking should be done on the forward side of all the frames forward of the mid ship frame and the aft side of the aft frames.

25.

The centres of the frame sections are removed using a power fretsaw. As can be seen in the previous photographs, holes were drilled through the frames to thread the saw blade through. To do this, just release the tension and lift the pin-ended blade out of its grooves and thread the frames on. You can also use a little vibrating fretsaw, cheap and cheerful and extremely accurate, but excruciatingly slow, and a lot of fiddling around is required when changing blades. Incidentally, for clarity's sake I have not shown the foot that holds the work piece down in this photograph. In practice it is necessary to use it, though I ended trimming most of it away so that I could get my fingers close enough to manoeuvre the blanks. Note also the sheet of wood beneath the section which is held in place with some double-sided tape and provides a better support while cutting.

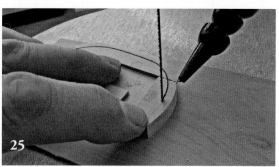

26.

Frame sections at various stages of completion. These are from forward on the hull and were mostly cut out as doubles.

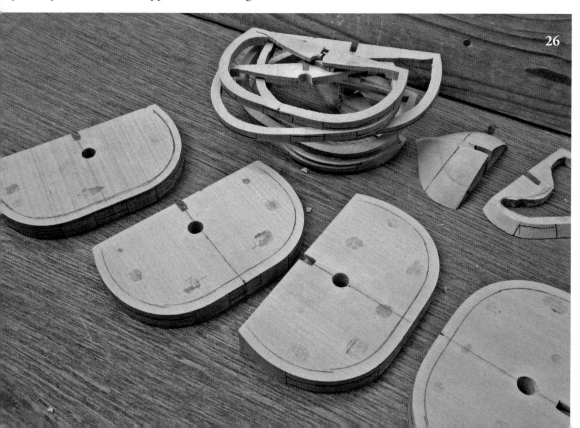

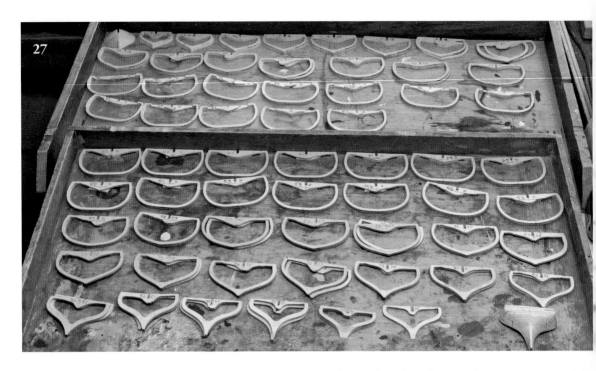

27.

All the frames have had their centres removed and have been laid out in doubles, or pairs. Other than the midship frames, which were assembled using Superglue (see photograph 9), many have separated while being cut out. Now they all need separating, the midship frames into their original double configuration and the remainder into singles. These single frames now need to be permanently glued into doubles, other than those at the extreme stern of the ship that will be fitted to the deadwood rather than the keel (see photograph 38). For this job, I use an aliphatic wood glue, applied only, as before, to those areas of the frame where the top timbers, futtocks and floors abut one another. They should be assembled back on the building jig during this process to ensure that everything lines up as it should, and they are then clamped or put under pressure while setting (see photograph 33).

28.

At this stage I like to re-mark the depth of the frames where necessary and then clean up the inner edge on this little sander.

29.

The sander is simply one of my Minicraft drills fitted with a drum sander and mounted beneath a plank with a hole in it. I assembled it temporarily for this job. Usually the drill on its stand is mounted horizontally on the right of my workbench, and is used for turning capstans, spars etc.

30.

The task now is to remove the unwanted timber from between the top timbers and floors on one of the doubled frames, which is a satisfying and easy process when using the technique shown here. The table saw has been set to exactly the depth of a single frame and the frame run over the blade just outside the line for top timbers and floors. The waste wood should just fall away.

31.

The frame can now be flipped over and the section between the futtocks removed.

32.

The result is a perfect double frame with the alternating floors and futtocks.

33.

When all the frames have been given this treatment, assembly of the hull can begin, again using wood glue and, of course, the building jig. After every three or four frames are added they should be clamped or put under pressure. In this photograph, the building jig is propped at an angle and a couple of wood wedges superglued to the weight to stop it rolling off.

34.

As the assembly proceeds the inside of the hull is cleaned up and the bevels on the frames on the insides of the frames established using the drum sander.

35.

As the job moves towards bow and stern, progressively smaller tools are needed. This carbide burr is useful at this stage.

36.

The bow section is also hollowed out before fitting.

37.

Here is the bow structure completed. Clamping is not easy here so elastic bands or, as here, a length of thin bungee cord should be used.

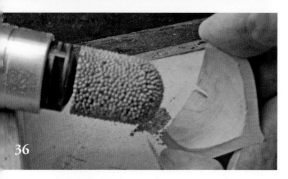

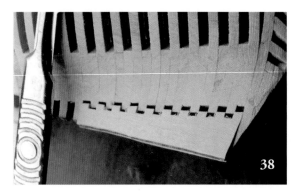

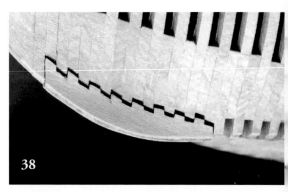

38

38

38.

An ingenious method of constructing the deadwood was invented by Donald McNarry and, with the use of veneer, makes the almost impossibly difficult task of creating the impression of a single piece of timber quite manageable. These two photographs are not of *Royal George* but of an earlier model of *Centurion* but

I include them to illustrate the stern and bow deadwood on a Navy Board model. In both photographs, the deadwood is partly withdrawn for demonstration purposes, when pushed home there are no gaps showing. On the original *Royal George* model, however, the deadwood is shown only at the stern, and this seems to have been the convention with most First Rates.

39.

39.

Now, to return to our model of *Royal George*. These are the frames that I have left as singles. They have been clamped in the jig and the position of the deadwood drawn in clearly with pencil. The depths of the cuts are also marked. Before unclamping and separating them they are numbered along the top.

40.

40.

Using a card jig, the area to be removed has been marked in on both sides of the frame. The angle is not critical and these lines are there only as a guide. What is critical is to cut to the lines marked on the outside of the frame in photograph 39.

41.

41.

The frames have been separated and one at a time they are put in a vice and the marked section carefully cut away from the frame with a fine razor saw.

42.

When this has been done, the pieces that have been removed are put on one side. Now the frames, glued up in pairs as before, are added to the hull as shown here.

43.

The last two frames to go into place. Note the fashion piece is not fitted at this stage.

44.

Now the segments that were removed are one by one slotted back into place gluing each to the previous one. I used small amounts of Superglue for this job because they must not adhere to the hull itself.

45.

They should be periodically prised free to ensure that they are not glued to the hull anywhere.

46.

All the segments have been glued together including the segment that is the lower section of the still-absent fashion piece, and a strip of box has been temporarily glued along the top for strength and to use as a handle.

47.

The next job is to reduce the sides of the deadwood by about 1/32in, so mark this in with a fine pencil.

48.

The deadwood is now grooved with 1/32in grooves using this dental burr.

49.

And then sanded down to the lines and flush with the base of the grooves. When it is back in place on the model it looks like this.

50.

Two strips of veneer or very thin box, as I have chosen to use here, are glued either side of the deadwood. With its curves and angles, this is easier said than done. I boiled the strips and then managed to put a twist into them while drying them off in front of a hair drier. They were then glued up with wood glue, bound with wire, and then a dowel was inserted either side to enforce the concave curve and the elastic band added for good measure.

51.

When dry, the veneer has to be very carefully trimmed exactly to the edge of the deadwood using a fine sharp scalpel blade. It can then be glued in place on the model along with the fashion piece and lightly sanded.

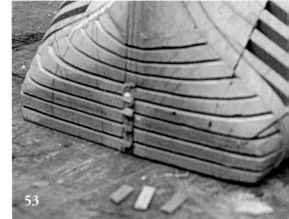

52.

Finally, the stern is reassembled. Each of the transoms are glued in place and scraps of the veneer originally used as spacers set between them though not glued in place this time.

53.

The transoms and filling piece have been fitted. The position of the sternpost has been marked and strips of boxwood have been glued between the transoms. These will represent the part of the sternpost that should be let into the transoms. The sternpost can now be glued and dowelled directly to the transoms and filling piece.

54.

At this stage, it is good practice to rub down and re-tape the longitudinal lines on the hull and then, using a sharp, pointed scalpel, trim the top timbers and floors where any slight deviations from the original have occurred. Something that in theory should not need doing, but little defects are inevitable.

55.

The model is turned over and the transverse timbers removed. I use a little Minicraft circular saw blade mounted on a mandrel, and it is best done with little chopping moves, so as to prevent the blade from binding.

56.

The inside edges can now be cleaned up with the drum sander.

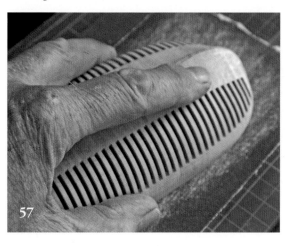

57.

The top edge also will probably need levelling, and this is best done on sandpaper laid over a sheet of glass.

58.

Many years ago, when building my first Navy Board hull, I reached this stage of the work and then fitted the keel and keelson. The following day I found I had a distorted hull, which had been brought about by atmospheric changes; these had caused the cross grain of the frames to swell at a greater rate than the longitudinal grain of the keel – the result was hogging. It took quite a bit of sorting out. Now I fit a timber along the top of the frames at the same time as the keel. It is shown here cut out, oversize, and ready to be fitted.

59.

60.

59.

The keel is now prepared and is here having the rabbet for the planking introduced. This is simply done by scraping with a sharp knife.

60.

Now the keel and the timber running round the top of the frames are glued up at the same time and placed under pressure to dry.

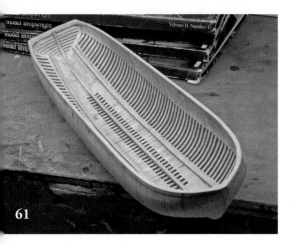

61.

62.

61.

With a permanently stabilised and very strong structure to work on, the inside of the hull is given a final clean up and then the keelson and stringers along the doublings can be fitted. Either ends of the keelson are made up of several layers of timber; I used holly because it takes a curve so well. This makes a very strong unit that places no strain on the hull.

62.

I like to dowel the key structures on a model, though I try to avoid areas where they will be noticed. They are rarely in evidence on the full-scale Navy Board models. I think the clean uncluttered runs of planking on these models is part of their unique charm, and at a miniature scale dowelling can appear quite overpowering. This photograph shows the keel / keelson assembly being drilled right through on the drill press. The timber round the top of the frames is treated in a similar manner.

63.

The dowels that I use are made by splitting a length of bamboo into progressively finer strips with a sharp knife. One end of a strip is then inserted through a draw plate held in a vice and pulled through successively smaller holes until the desired size is reached. My 'draw plate' is in fact a drill gauge that has seen many years service. It will produce dowels down to No. 60. For smaller sizes, I make my own from tin plate. The dowels are dipped in wood glue, inserted and then cut or broken off.

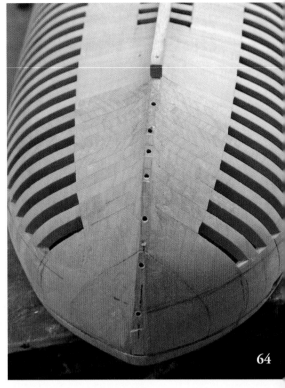

65.

The template used to mark in the wales has had the lower-deck gun ports cut out so that they can be marked out on the hull. Care needs to be taken to ensure that the station lines being marked on the hull line up with those on the template.

64.

These holes have been drilled to dowel the stem to the frames at a later date. When the stem is finally fitted they can be re-drilled from the inside to pass only a short distance through the stem.

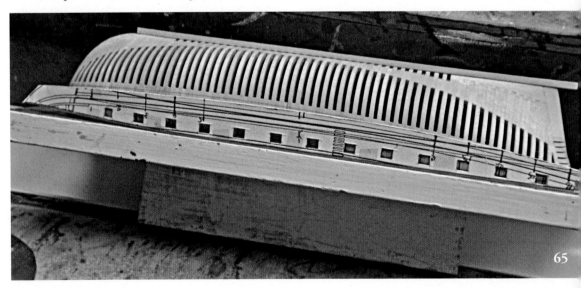

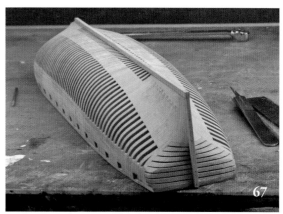

66.

67.

The ports are now drilled and then cut out with a sharp scalpel.

The sternpost has been glued and dowelled in place and the whole model given a final clean up.

68.

The upperworks, above the lower deck, display no exposed frames and for this part of the model a single piece of jelutong was cut to size and a template was prepared for the remaining section of the ship's profile. This was cut 1/8in short at the bottom to allow for another boxwood layer to be inserted, which is explained shortly (see photograph 71).

70.

Using chisel and plane, the top can then be levelled to the depth of the cuts. I should emphasise that this is merely the way I am went about this task on this particular model. If you are without a bandsaw or most of the other pieces of machinery that I now use don't be put off; hand tools are just as good, though the task will certainly take longer.

69.

When trimming the upper hull to size on the bandsaw I cut it somewhat oversize before running it up against the saw blade like this. The set square ensures that the block is kept at right angles to the saw table while small cuts are made down to the top of the marked profile all along the length of the block.

71.

With previous Navy Board models, I glued the upper and lower body together before going on to carve the hull to shape. Never having tackled a three decker before I felt it would be a great advantage to be able to gain easier access to the lower and middle deck while fitting out, so I determined to find a way of dowelling the two halves together so that they could easily be separated until it became essential to finally join them. This also meant that the upper body could, for the most part, be carved, and the upper deck fitted, while separate from the framed section. The layer of box to which the upper part of the model will be attached later is in the foreground.

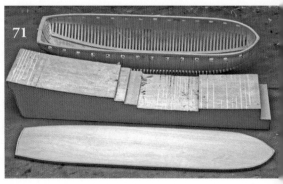

72.

The next task is to mark on the gun ports. The template used for the broadside of the upper hull has had all of the gun ports cut out and has been pinned in place while they are all marked in.

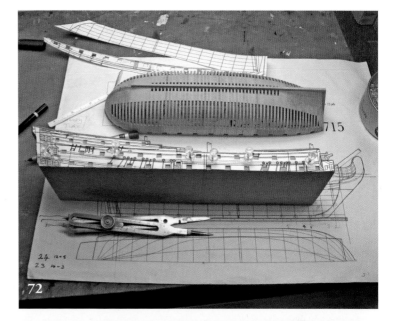

73.

74.

The ports are now going to all be centrally drilled, but in order to do this accurately the hull needs to be consistently held at right angles to the drill table. As an aid to this, two squares of MDF can be glued to the bottom of the model. A small spray of Superglue accelerator is applied to the base of the model and a blob of thick Superglue to the centre of the edge of one of the squares. The hull is then held at right angles to the work surface while the square is fixed to the base of the block to the model; the glue will set almost instantly.

When all of the ports have been drilled, the squares are broken free and the same procedure carried out on the other side of the hull.

75.

Templates are also used to mark in the plan of the upper section. This can be cut out on the band saw, and then, as shown here, the excess timber trimmed away.

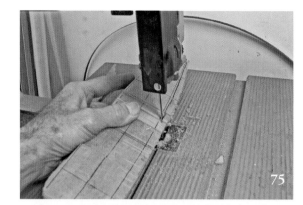

76.

For the dowelling together of the two layers of the model the centre of the boxwood sheet is removed. At this point, I realised that it should have been have been cut a little longer at the stern to form part of the transom, so I glued on a couple of pieces of jelutong. It is all too easy to make these little mistakes but they are easily remedied with scraps of wood and a tube of Superglue.

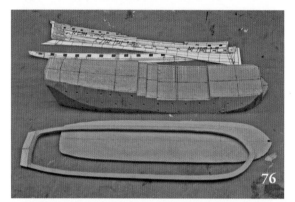

77.

Next, the boxwood layer is temporarily glued to the frames with a few spots of Seccotine. Behind the model can be seen a simple support for the hull – a couple of batons glued down the centre that locate tightly either side of the keel and two blocks of wood that support the hull on either side. Care must be taken to ensure that the hull sits absolutely upright in the support. Seated on the support, the hull is now taken to the drill press and holes drilled down through both boxwood layers.

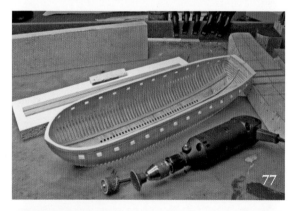

78.

I drilled these holes between each of the gun ports but I think this was unnecessary; half as many would have been quite adequate. Once the holes have been drilled, the boxwood layer can be prized free and bamboo dowels glued in the holes in the lower section as shown.

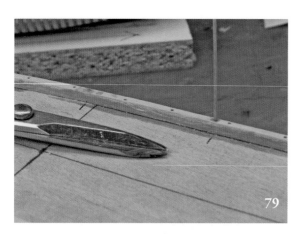

79.

The boxwood layer is lined up on the underside of the top section and glued and dowelled permanently in place.

80.

The upper and lower sections can easily be separated and reassembled at will.

81.

A new set of templates of the body of the ship have been prepared and with a chisel, gouge and the little violin maker's plane the upper hull can carved to the correct shape.

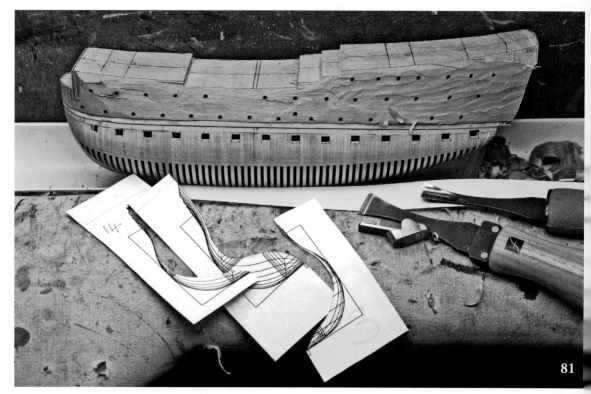

82.

83.

The final work is done with a variety of sanding blocks. I find that periodically marking in the station lines on the hull is helpful at this stage of the work.

A template should also be prepared for the stern. It is important to check with the plans at this point and ensure that this outer surface of the stern, as shown here, will fit neatly just inside the outer stern windows on all four decks.

84.

The first rough shaping nearing completion.

85.

The two sections of the hull are now separated and the core timber of the upper section removed on the bandsaw.

84

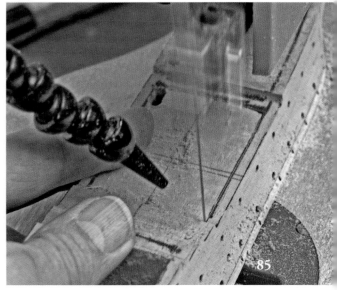

85

86.

Leave a couple of struts between the sides to give support and strength to the whole structure. They will be retained, in part at least, for as long as they don't impede the work.

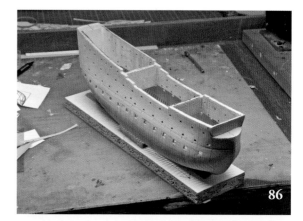

87.

The inside of the hull can now be shaped, as here from above and then, with the lower section removed, from below.

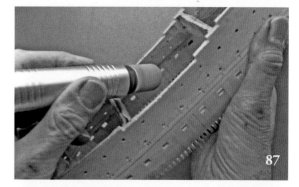

88.

As an aid to marking in the gun ports and ensuring a nice clean run fore and aft, I made up some double-thickness Sellotape which was then cut slightly narrower than the depth of each run of ports and, using the drilled holes as guides, stretched along the hull. The top and bottom of each port was then marked in.

89.

Using the broadside template, the sides of the gun ports can be marked in. The top of the model (the underside of the uppermost capping rails) can also be remarked at this stage.

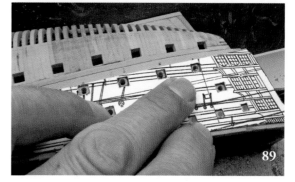

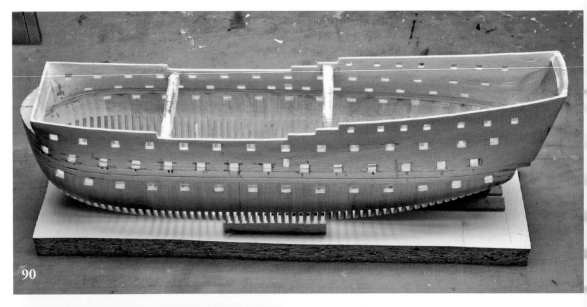

90

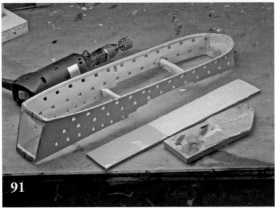

91

92

90.

Use a scalpel to trim the gun ports to size, and then re-sand both inside and out until satisfied with the thickness of the walls. A visual check is easily made once the ports have been pierced, exposing the thickness of the sides at any point.

91.

Being able to remove the topsides makes this task so much easier because access and vision are clear from all sides.

92.

The stem of the model is formed from two separate pieces of wood. The first of these to be made and fitted is the apron and it must be cut to fit to the bow exactly. I cut it first of all from a tracing taken from the plans, then offered it up to the bow, and finally remarked it and sand with the drum sander mounted under the little wooden table.

93.

The apron is then cut from the sheet of box, squaring and neatening up the outside edge on the disk sander.

94.

It is then glued to the lower section only of the hull and elastic bands are fitted round a spar passed through the lower gun ports.

95.

The stem itself is then prepared, again using a tracing from the plans. It is possible to hold it just behind the apron while marking with a sharp pencil, which gives a really accurate line to sand.

96.

97.

96.

Then, very slowly and very carefully, sand to the line. Although this line has to be finished very accurately, the stem itself should be cut oversize to allow for later trimming.

97.

Photograph 64 shows holes being drilled for the dowelling of the stem to the model. I decided that a few more dowels would not go amiss and the drilling was done through both apron and hull.

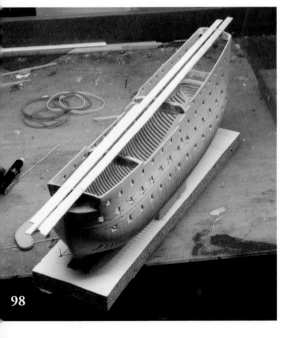

98

99

98.

Two strips of scrap timber have been tacked in place with Superglue either side of the centreline; these will act as supports for the stem while gluing it in place.

99.

The stem is glued in place, and the supports ensure that it is set dead in line with the centreline of the model.

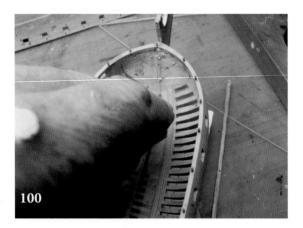

100.

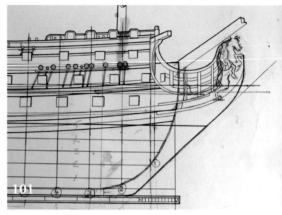

101.

100.

The holes that were drilled (in photograph 97) are now re-drilled from the inside, well into the stem. Bamboo dowels are then dipped in wood glue and pushed firmly into them before breaking or cutting them off flush with the hull. When they are all in place, a sanding disk or burr can be used to level the ends.

101.

After fitting the stem, it is trimmed to its final size. Another template is used for this, made from stiff tracing paper and taking the dimensions directly from the plans. Before doing this it is a good idea to sketch in the main components of the figurehead to help with the cutting of the stem. Good photographic reference of the model on which the miniature is being based is invaluable.

102.

The stem marked out from the template.

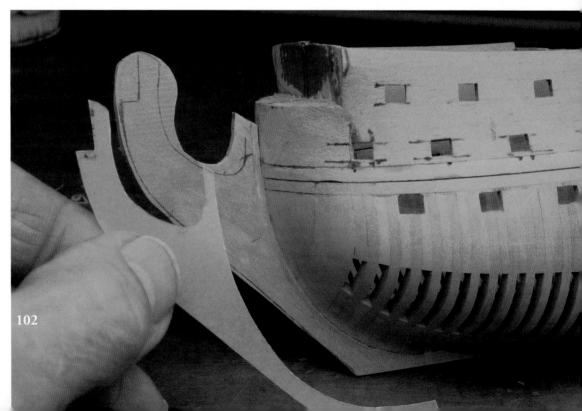

103.

Now the stem is tapered gently towards the top, from about a scale thickness of 18in at the foot to 10in to 12in at the top. This can be started with the disk sander but should then be brought to a fine finish with sanding boards

104.

The final task on the carcass is the forming of the lower transom. A piece of jellutong has been shaped to fit around the stern and sternpost. It is glued in place but to the framed section only.

105.

The transom is then carved to shape and the stern gun ports and the helm port for the rudder pierced.

103

104

105

106

107

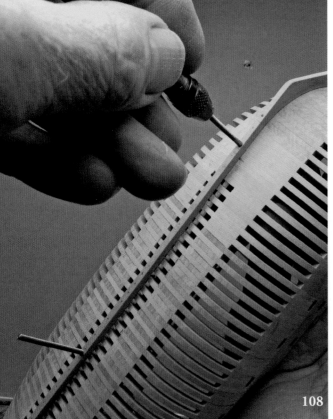

108

106.

While shaping the transom, as well as keeping a close check on the height and projection from the sternpost, I keep a further check on its symmetry by measuring back from a set point on the keel to each corner.

107.

Its now time to make a decision about the mounting and displaying of the model. Various options are available, and I usually opt for cradles of one sort or another, but for *Royal George* it was decided to mount her on three turned pillars and support the hull either side with brass struts. This was, in fact, the most commonly used method of presentation for models of this period. Holes are being drilled for the stainless steel threaded rod that will be inserted through keel, frames, keelson and turned pillars to secure the model to the plinth.

108.

The holes are drilled to a slightly smaller diameter than the threaded steel rod. Each section of rod is then cut to the required length, fitted firmly in a pin vice, and screwed into the model.

It is now time to set the model on one side and think about the layout and construction of the decks and their fittings. This is not quite such a straightforward task as it might seem because there are no plans available for *Royal George* or any other ships of her class. So I had to rely on information gleaned from the contemporary models of *Royal George* and *Royal William* with some reference to other Navy Board models of the period. But here again nothing is straightforward because there are considerable differences in the way the decks of these models are framed and laid out. There is certainly a view that it is preferable to build copies of existing Navy Board models rather than base models on plans of actual named ships because the scale construction patterns have been made for you. However, with this model I did not slavishly follow the deck layout of the Boston *Royal George*, partly because I do not have sufficient detailed information on the model and partly because there are many features that are at considerable variance with the two models of *Royal William*, as well as with the contemporary engraving of the ship, the plans, and the established ship and model building practices of the period.

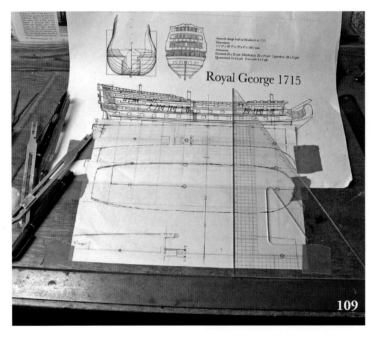

109.

First, it is necessary to make a plan. The ship's profile is taped to the bench and a clean sheet of paper taped beneath it. Now the line of the midship frame is extended downwards to the bottom of the sheet of paper and the steel straight edge in the foreground fixed to the bench with double-sided tape. This must be set exactly at right angles to the centreline that I have just drawn and parallel with the keel of the ship. The photograph shows the first rough draught taking shape. Lines have been drawn across the paper at right angles to the centreline that represent the

centre of each of the decks. Now, using the set square, the extreme ends of the decks can be established and also the position of the masts on each deck. Constantly referring to photos of the contemporary models, the positions of hatches and deck beams are worked out along with those for capstans, bitts and pumps. You must also determine the exact position for the break of the forecastle, quarterdeck and poop, keeping in mind the gun ports of the deck below as any gangways and ladders must be well clear of them. There is no need to draw in the perimeter of each deck because the positions of all the above are marked along the centreline.

110.

The deck beams are cut from strips of boxwood, pre-shaped for the camber which, incidentally, increases as you move up the ship and the decks become narrower. So, separate formers need to be prepared for the different decks; then the strips of wood from which the beams are to be cut are boiled for a minute or so before being clamped to the formers. They should be left to dry in a warm, airy place for several days. Individual deck beams can than be sliced off these strips as required.

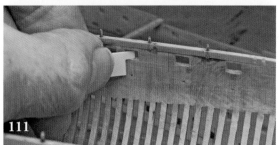

111.

Before starting to fit the beams, the deck clamps will need to be fitted, and here a plastic card jig is being used to mark in the distance between the top edge of the clamp and the lower edge of the gun ports.

112.

I find the easiest way to fit the deck clamps is to fix them, as shown here, using ordinary clothes pegs. Once firmly in place and any minor adjustments made, some very thin Superglue can be applied to the top of the clamp where it will penetrate the join and secure it in place.

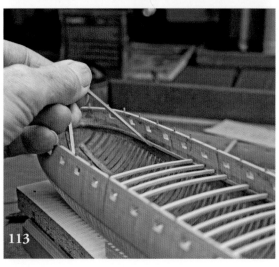

113.

The clamps are in place and the inboard surfaces of the frames have been varnished with a matt finish polyurethane to which I added small quantities of raw umber and burnt sienna artist's oil colour to give the wood a deeper and richer look. Upon careful inspection of the photograph it will be seen where I have marked the midship frame line both inside and outside of the hull. By referring to the deck plans and working fore and aft from this reference point the positions of all the deck beams can be marked in pencil just above the clamp. The deck beams have been sliced from the pre-shaped strips of box and are being fitted. The little dividers are ideal for measuring the length of each beam.

114.

The shaped half beams to be fitted just fore and aft of the mainmast are easily formed using a sanding drum.

115.

All of the main beams have been fitted and spacers glued between them by way of masts and capstans. The spacer with the cross on it is only temporary and was glued in place with just a couple of spots of Seccotine. The two lines of the cross establish the position of the centreline and midship frame. Measuring fore and aft from the centre frame, the positions of masts and capstans can be located and drilled accordingly. When this has been done the spacer is broken free. The same procedure will be carried out for each of the three gun decks.

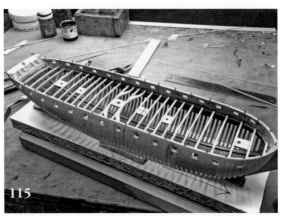

116.

The next task is to fit spacers between the beams where they join the decks, gluing them onto the top of the clamps. These will become the supports for the ledges so they need to be made the thickness of the beams minus the thickness of the ledges.

117.

The next task is the fitting of the carlings. A batten of wood, from which the carlings would later be cut, had some double-sided tape applied to one side. This was then laid fore and aft along the deck to establish the position of the carlings. A fair run is needed approximately midway between the centreline and hull side. A line was then marked in on either side, on each of the beams. Now, with the batten removed, small angled joints, or scores as they are more properly called, are cut on both sides of each beam to accept the ends of each of the carlings. This can be done using a sliver of razor saw blade mounted in a pin vice.

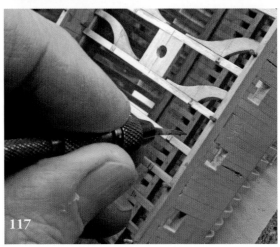

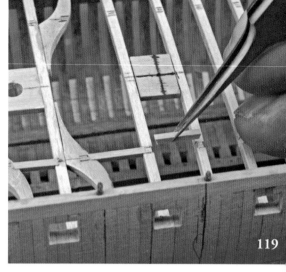

118.

The centres can be removed with a scalpel.

119.

Sections of carling can now be cut to size and a little wood glue applied to the ends before fitting them firmly in their scores.

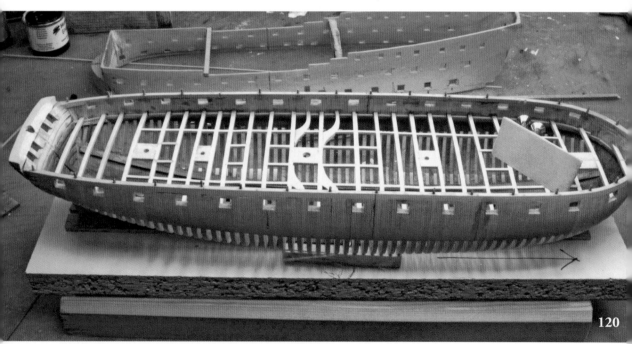

120.

When all of the carlings have been fitted, the whole structure is given a rub down with the sanding block shown on the right. There are a couple of screws in the top of the block to make it easier to hold and the edges of the block are slightly rounded to alleviate any tendency to catch on any of the delicate timbers.

The Decks 57

121.

122.

Two shelves have been fitted between the beams. They are made to be an accurate fit and are glued in place with wood glue, the final height being established and checked with the jig.

123.

Either side of the hatch openings shelves cut from the ledge material are fitted, again using the jig.

Fitting the ledges can seem a daunting prospect, particularly on a three-decker. But in reality it takes a lot less time than you would expect and it is very satisfying to see the intricate and complex deck taking shape. Before making a start, however, provision has to be made for fitting them. On a full-size Navy Board model long carlings would be fitted either side of the hatches and the ledges would be scored into them. On this model I am going to simplify things by fitting various shelves on which the ends of the ledges can rest. To this end I have made this little jig, largely self explanatory, but the strip of timber glued across the end of the underside is a piece of the boxwood that I had prepared for the ledges.

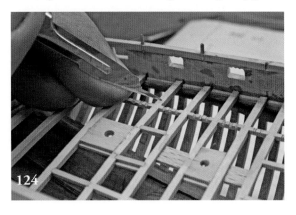

124.

Scores have to be cut in the carlings for the ledges and this is most easily accomplished with a sharply pointed scalpel.

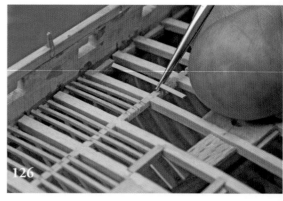

125.

126.

The scores are then cleaned up with a fine needle file.

Fitting the ledges. Before gluing each ledge in place it is given a slight curve by hand to correspond with the camber of the deck. As can be seen one end of each of the ledges locates in a score on the carling while the other rests on and is glued to one of the shelves where it will later be covered by a section of decking.

127.

With the job finished the deck can be given another clean up with the little sanding block.

128.

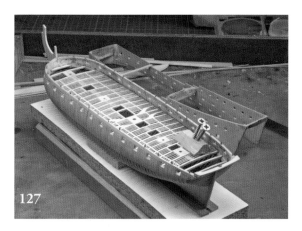

127

It's now time to fit the deck planking. Original Navy Board models are invariably decked with either plain boards or boards with the planking marked on them. For this model I used the latter, made up from yellow cedar shavings mounted on cartridge paper that has been pre-stretched on a drawing board. Stretching paper is a simple and very useful procedure that will ensure that it remains absolutely flat even after being treated with water-based paint or glue. To stretch the paper it is first of all well wetted either by running it under a tap or by using a sponge. It is then laid flat on the board, smoothed flat by hand and the edges taped to the board with brown Gumstrip sealing tape. As it dries the paper tautens like a drum skin

and even if it is subsequently moistened it will once again dry flat. Incidentally, the drawing board needs to be made of wood as the Gumstrip will not stick to the modern white Melamine ones. The shavings and the paper are treated with a liberal coat of Seccotine which is allowed to become tacky before mounting the shavings.

128

129.

I bedded these down using a veneer hammer, although a piece of smooth wood or a roller would do just as well.

130.

The paper has been removed from the drawing board and mounted, with Sellotape, on a sheet of chipboard. At the far end of the board a ruler marked out in sixteenths of an inch has been clamped to the board with a batten of wood. Now the shavings are scored with the craft knife, moving the set square a sixteenth at a time. When the required number of shavings have been scored, they are given a coat of lightly stained varnish; this will darken the scored lines and act as a priming coat. They can then be set on one side ready for use on the model.

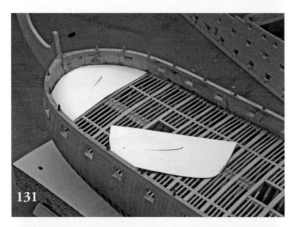

131.

I decided to plank the end sections of the lower and middle gun decks, which will, on the finished model, be all but invisible. Shown here are the two paper templates for the end sections of this deck.

132.

Short lengths of planking were joined edge to edge with Superglue on a non-stick paper surface. Then, using the templates, the deck ends were cut to shape and can be seen here glued to the beams, again using Superglue. Also fitted is the central run of planking, which had hatch openings roughly removed and undersized holes drilled for the masts and capstans. Before fitting it, I drew pencil lines across beams and ledges just inside where the edge of the strip would come. This was used as a guide for applying the Superglue that was applied to both beams and carlings with a wire. Starting from one end about a third of the planking was glued down at one time. Card templates for the side planking are shown here, and when the strips for the side planking have been cut to size they are glued down in exactly the same way.

133.

The main bitts have been made and fitted. This is a relatively simple task with the various components cut from boxwood. The only features not visible in the photographs are the round spigots carved on the ends of the upright posts for insertion in holes drilled in the deck. A strip of mounted shaving has been cut and fitted round the bulwarks adjacent to the deck, which represents the thicker planking or 'stringers'; it gives a neat seal between the deck and bulwarks. These have been given a couple of coats of dark red paint.

134.

At this stage it is a good plan to make the six capstans required for the three decks. There are only two fitted on the lower deck, so the others can be put on one side until required. On the finished model only one of them will be readily visible so the other five are not intended to be fully detailed. It is always difficult to know just how much detail to add when the item will be invisible on the final model. I try to tread a middle path. In the present instance, the capstans and bitts below decks may just be glimpsed as shadowy objects through the gun ports once the remaining decks have been fitted so any fine detail would not be discernable. This approach is not without precedent for some of the original models were fitted with very simple 'dummy' capstans below decks. First, six drums, like those shown here, are turned from some suitable hard wood. The drum is the diameter of the drumhead and the depth of the drum represents the overall height of the capstan. The spigots will serve to mount them in the drill chuck for turning and, when finally shortened, for fitting them into the deck.

135.

The barrel and drumhead are shaped with a carbide burr, and then finished it off with a needle file.

136.

137.

Next, it is mounted in a pin vice and the whelps fitted, which, at this stage, are left rectangular. Then for the fore jeer capstan the chock pieces are fitted.

The chock pieces can be simply sliced from a strip of boxwood with a knife.

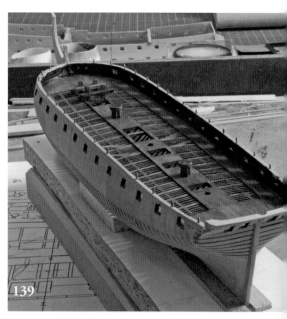

138.

139.

The final turning takes place in the drill chuck. It can be started with a sanding disk or diamond burr mounted in another drill and finished with a needle file. Holes for the capstan bars can also be drilled at this stage.

The completed deck with bitts and capstan fitted. All the planking is in place and the edges of the hatch openings have been trimmed back to the beams and carlings. Two more coats of the stained varnish have been applied.

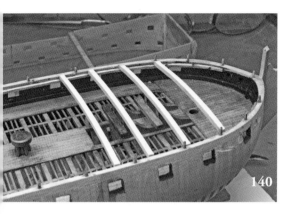

140.

141.

Now, for almost a repeat performance to fit the middle gun deck. It should be a somewhat simpler and more straightforward project using the experience gained fitting the lower deck. In addition, the split hull method makes the fitting of the beam shelf easier and access better.

The work in progress. The extent of the decking to be fitted has been marked on the beams and the batten resting on top of them is temporarily held in place with double-sided tape and is being used to establish the position of the carlings. The beams are then marked with pencil either side of the batten; the starboard batten has been removed and the pencil lines can be clearly seen.

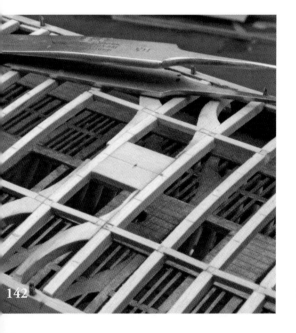

142.

143.

The half beams and the carlings being fitted.

Once the framing is completed, the upper section of the hull is fitted temporarily in place while card templates for the decking are prepared.

144

144

The decking cut to size and glued to the beams. Once the glue has set, the upper section of the hull can be removed before fitting capstans and hatch coamings.

145.

Now the upper section is returned and fitted firmly in place while fixing the stringers. This needs doing with care, for they must only be glued to the side of the ship and not to the deck.

146.

Before fitting the beam shelves for the upper deck, I made few little clamps from some old clothes pegs. They were roughly trimmed on the bandsaw.

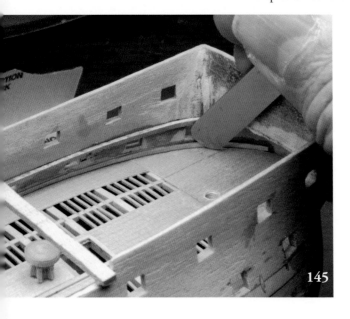

145

146

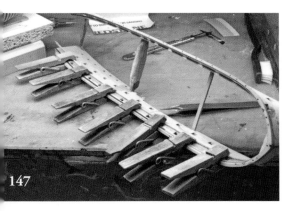

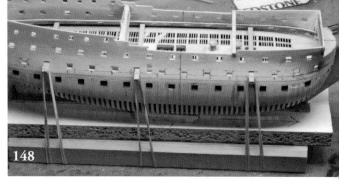

147.

The pegs hold the beam shelf in place ready for the application of the Superglue.

149.

The rest of the work on the upper deck can be carried out with the top section removed. This will once again make the work that much easier, and, again, it is a repetition of the work carried out on the lower and middle decks.

148.

With the stringers and beam shelves fitted, the upper section of the model is replaced and three strips of wood have been threaded through middle gun ports and elastic bands used to pull the two sections tightly together. These will not be removed until all the upper deck beams have been firmly glued in place. This is to ensure that no warping of the upper section occurs.

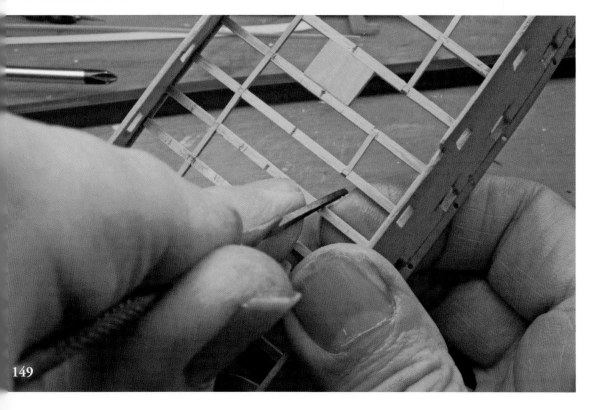

∽ Gratings and Deck Fittings ∽

There is no reason why brass etched gratings could not be used for the model; I have used them myself on a number of occasions. If you do decide to use them they will need painting with a natural wood colour before being given several coats of the same stain as used for the decks. If you have an airbrush this is absolutely the best way of doing it.

For this model, I intended to make scale wooden gratings and the one absolutely essential tool for this task is an accurate miniature table saw. With one of these, all that is then required are a few scraps of boxwood and a fair degree of time and patience.

150.

151.

Before making a start on the gratings a 12 thou blade was fitted to the saw and a sheet of boxwood fixed to the top of the saw table to provide a new work surface that must be a tight fit either side of the blade. A strip of double-sided tape is applied to the underside of the near end of the wood and, with the edge held against the fence, a cut is made half way through before switching off the saw and bedding it down onto the metal surface.

Next, a strip of boxwood, 12 thou square, must be prepared and glued to the boxwood base exactly 12 thou away from the blade, which has now been set to cut to a depth of 12 thou. Now a sheet of wood approximately 24 thou thick is passed over the saw using the strip of wood as a fence to cut out a groove.

152.

Then a second cut is made, this time passing the sheet over the strip of wood, ensuring that the first groove runs along the strip which thus serves as a guide.

153.

Progressive cuts are made in this way until the far side of the sheet is reached and the underside looks like this.

154.

Now you need to prepare enough 12 thou square stuff to complete the gratings. If you multiply the length of each of the cuts made in the sheet by the number of cuts made this will give you the amount that you'll need. As you can see here I am again using a temporary boxwood surface that allows for the lengths to be cut 12 thou square.

155.

Using the same set up as shown in the previous photograph, strips can now be taken from the grooved sheet. First, the grooved side should be covered with a low tack masking tape and should be cut with the taped side down; this will prevent damage while sawing. Cut one strip at a time – this is very important – before mounting it as shown in the following photograph, so that the strips are reassembled in exactly the sequence in which they were removed from the stock. If jumbled up, the tiny variations in angle and distance, which are the inevitable outcome of the sawing process, will make the laying up of the grating pretty well impossible.

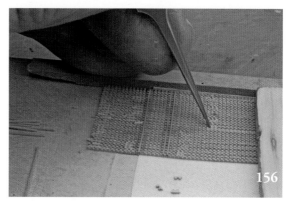

156.

The laying up process is under way. To the left of the picture a strip of double-sided tape has been fixed to the board and at the back a batten of timber has been glued to it; beneath the strips I have positioned a sheet of non-stick paper. Now, one strip at a time, the grooved material is mounted as shown, placing short spacers of the same material between each strip. When two rows of spacers have been fitted, one or two of the 12 thou battens can be glued in place. The right hand row of spacers can be slid further to the right before fitting another batten.

157.

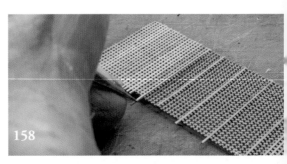

158.

The process is repeated until the other end of the gratings is reached. I find a strip of wood pegged as shown, just ahead of the work, helps to keep the structure stable while it is worked on.

Now all that remains to do is to glue up and insert the remaining battens.

159.

160.

A light sand over …

… should be followed by a clean up with a bristle brush, and if you don't have one of these, give an old toothbrush a close haircut.

161.

162.

The gratings have been cut to size (fractionally larger than the openings in the deck) and glued in place.

Now the hatch coamings are assembled around them. The triangular inserts in the coaming for the stairwell will be rounded off with a diamond burr.

163.

The ladders leading down from the upper deck to the middle and from the middle to the lower are all double, not easy fittings to construct in miniature if separate

treads are fitted either side of the central runner; so I am going to fit a false runner after assembling the ladder. The strips of wood worked on have been prepared with the grain running across them so that a central groove can be cut using a 12 thou blade.

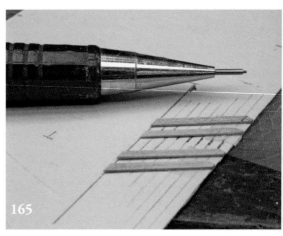

164.

The individual treads can now be sliced from their ends.

165.

The distance between treads and overall height of the ladders has been marked on a piece of card and one side of each of the four ladders has been fitted to the card with double-sided tape. The positions of the treads can then be marked on them.

166.

The treads are now glued in place and the metal square is used to check that the treads are set at right angles to the sides.

167.

When dry, the other sides are glued to the steps and a narrow runner glued in the central grooves. At the top of the ladder an extra sliver of wood is glued beneath the runner before trimming it to the same shape as the sides. The ladders can now be put to one side.

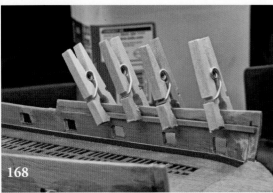

168.

169.

168.

The beam shelves for the fo'c's'le and quarterdeck should be fitted now.

169.

Then plank the inside of the bulwarks with some pre-painted and unmounted wood shaving. They extend half way up the side of the ports, which are then opened up with the scalpel.

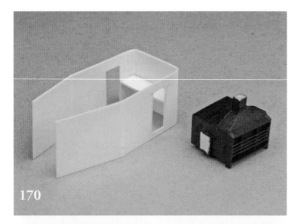

170

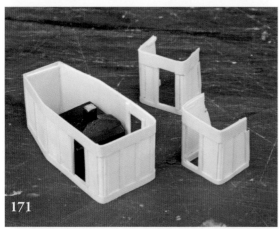

171

170.

There are a number of fittings that now have to be made and installed on the upper deck, and I have used, uncharacteristically, what can only be called a mixed-media approach. For much of this work I used Plasticard because it is ideally suited to the task. My only reservation about this material is its lifespan. I have used it occasionally over the last 35 years and still have some of my original stock left, and that which was stored away from ultraviolet light has shown no sign of deterioration. I would recommend that any fittings made from it should be given a blanket coat of matt black, preferably airbrushed, before applying the final colour. Here the partitions will be painted a light buff before receiving several coats of the stained varnish. This photograph shows the carcass for the galley under construction and a wood and wire brodie stove that has been partially detailed on those places that may be glimpsed on the finished model. The unpainted patch on the side is one of two small squares of wood fixed either side of the stove that will eventually be glued to the galley sides.

171.

The two small cabins that will be located either side of the upper deck beneath the forecastle and the galley. They have all been panelled with 10 thou Plasticard.

172.

173.

The two partitions fitted beneath the quarterdeck are a little more demanding to make, featuring curved surfaces, windows and doors. As some of the windows themselves are curved, they can be made from clear Plasticard. using jigs from some scrap wood. The clear plastic should be cut to size, laid over the opening and the wire grill in the background placed over it to prevent it curling up while warming it under the cooker grill. When sufficiently softened, the male mould is plunged partially through the opening and then removed after allowing a few seconds for the plastic to harden.

Three of the transparent castings and two intermediate castings, with openings cut out for the double doors, have been assembled. The transparent sections are in the process of being faced up with some 10 thou material. There is no pretending that this stage of the work is easy. There needs to be seemingly endless checking to ensure that the whole partition fits tightly to both deck and sides of the ship and that the centre section will fit neatly beneath a deck beam and the remainder be flush with the top of it.

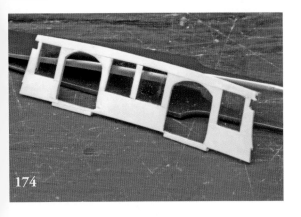

174.

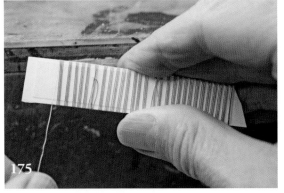

175.

The straight bulkhead fitted further aft is much simpler to make and fit. It is being made up here from a single piece of clear Plasticard faced up with 10 thou.

There are a number of decorative columns required for the partitions. I made these by binding tinned copper wire around some card, three strands for each, and flooding one side with very thin Superglue.

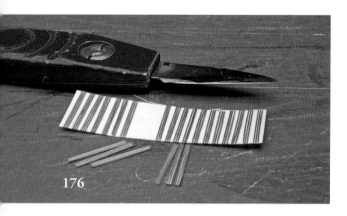

176.

When dry, the top and bottom of the card can be trimmed, allowing the wire on the reverse side to fall away and the individual columns parted off with a sharp knife.

177.

They can now be added to the partitions where required. The windows have an arched top and the easiest way to introduce this is to put several squares of Plasticard together and drill through them with an appropriately-sized bit and then cut each piece into quarters before finally trimming to size and fitting them to the partition.

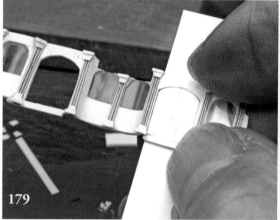

178.

The tops and bottoms of the columns are now finished off.

179.

Now doors are cut to fit the door openings and each marked so that they can be returned to the same position.

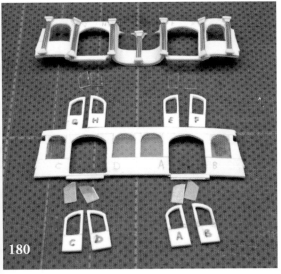

180.

The windows in the tops of the doors are drilled and cut out and clear panes cut to fit. These are then glued in place with just a touch of thin Superglue.

181.

A wire moulding has been glued over the door openings and both sides of the partitions have been given a coat of black acrylic followed by a couple of coats of natural wood colour. Some tissue paper has been painted the same colour on both sides and treated with the stained varnish. A piece can just be seen in the top left-hand corner of the picture. Strips are trimmed from this and used to construct the window frames. I use Seccotine for this job, but its hopelessly inefficient as an adhesive on the shiny plastic, so when the frames are finished all the windows are given a generous coat of gloss varnish.

182.

Finally, all the woodwork is given a couple of coats of the stain, and black paper panels fitted beneath the windows.

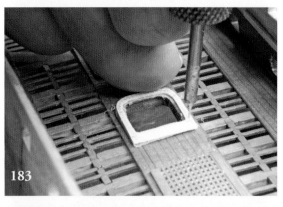

183.

There are two double ladders in evidence leading down from the upper deck. The aft ladders situated just beneath the break of the quarterdeck are surrounded by an ornamental balustrade and are the next fittings to be made. Again, you can use Plasticard. It has to be cut accurately to shape before securing it in place on the hatch coaming with double-sided tape. Then the positions of all the balusters are marked before drilling.

184.

The rail is now removed from the coaming and the supporting bar trimmed away. Lengths of wire are inserted and glued into the coamings, while strips of wood are used to ensure the rail is set at the correct height. When most of the wires are in place, it can be superglued to them and the wood removed. The remaining wires are then fitted and any protruding above the rail can be cut away and filed flush.

185.

The two ladders leading down from the upper deck are now fitted and glued in place as shown. This is carried out with the two sections of the model fitted tightly together. The aft ladder shown here is now fitted with the supports for a rail.

186

The hand rails were shaped from plastic rod and scraped to an oval section before bending to the required shape. One of the attributes of this rod is its ability to retain a sharp bend.

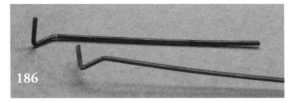

187.

The hand rails have been fitted and blended in with the top rail; I have also glued a strip of tissue paper over the ends of the wires, to hide them, with a liberal amount of Superglue before giving the whole structure a good rub down. To the left of the picture is the tip of a paint brush loaded with wood glue. This is used to build up the centres of the balusters.

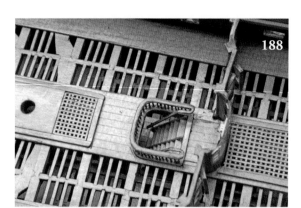

188.

The ensemble has been finished off with the necessary coats of paint and stain.

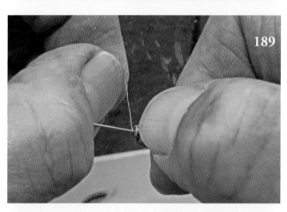

189.

Ring bolts on the upper deck should be made and fitted at this stage. There is no great mystery to their manufacture, just simple repetitive work. Those fitted to the bulwarks are formed around a drill shank, as can be seen in this photograph, whereas those fitted to the deck are simple rings cut from a spiral formed around a drill shank. In all, 220 are required.

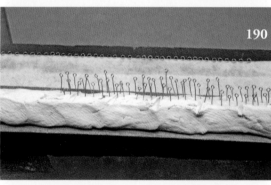

190.

I prefer to airbrush the ringbolts; here they are mounted in Plasticine prior to spraying. In the background, the simple rings are mounted, by their edge only, on low tack masking tape. This was fixed to the timber batten with the ever reliant double-sided tape.

191.

The bulwarks are drilled for the ring bolts.

192.

193.

When fitting the ringbolts to the deck, first of all drill and insert a wire pin in the deck. This is then cut off very short and the ring glued to both the pin and deck. A little blob of glue is then applied over the pin and ring and finally touched up with black paint.

All partitions and cabins are now fixed permanently to the deck and the beams for the forecastle and quarterdeck fitted. The beakhead bulkhead has been cut from thin ply but it has not yet been glued in position. The beams were finally given a rub down with the sanding block.

194.

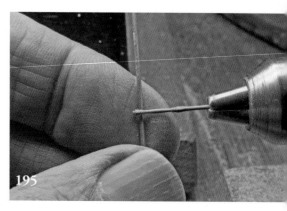

195.

The partitions and beams fitted for the quarterdeck.

There are two turned pillars to be fitted at the break of the forecastle and one beneath the quarterdeck. They were turned, as shown here, in a drill chuck.

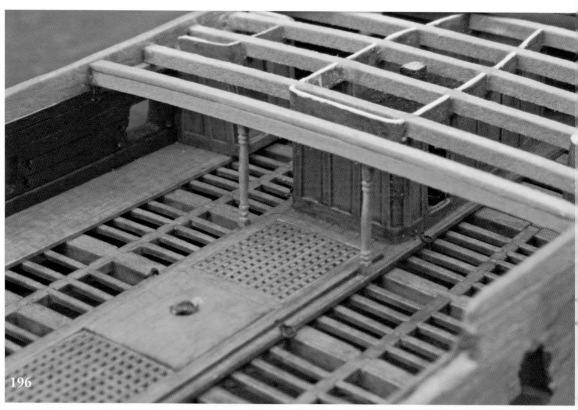

196.

Before fitting the pillars, I added an extra deck beam behind the beam positioned above them to add strength. It will not be visible on the finished model but it allowed me to drill through the beam and down into the deck for the fitting of the pillars from above. This was done in the drill press to ensure that the pillars are set vertical. Note also the completed ring bolts in the deck.

197.

The break of the quarterdeck with a clear view of the extra supporting beam and the margin plank to which the deck planking will butt up against.

198.

Before moving on to the deck planking, the bitts at the base of the mainmast need to be fitted. They have been left until now because the two beams carrying the central gangway to the mast will connect the foremost quarterdeck beam with the fore bitts. Having drilled holes, they are now being opened up with a square file so that the bitts may pass through the deck. Like the ladders, they will be glued in place with the two sections of the model firmly fitted together as they pass down to the deck below.

199.

Construction of the bitts was quite straightforward work. It was just important to ensure that the top of the fore bitts ends up exactly the same distance above the upper deck as the top of the quarterdeck.

All decorative work was carved with a knife, finishing any curves with a diamond burr. The gangway beams were fitted to the bitts and the quarterdeck with the same joint as was used for the carlings. Battens of wood have been fitted to the beams to support the gratings.

200.

The forecastle deck has been laid …

201.

… and the quarterdeck almost completed. Note the ornamentally shaped opening at the forward end of the deck. This feature was copied from one of the *Royal William* models.

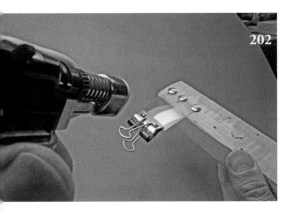

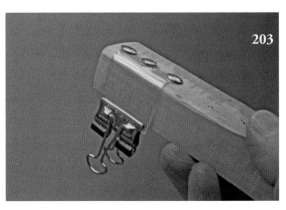

202.

There are some quite complex cabin partitions beneath the break of the poop deck, and once again curves are required. I used a different method to shape the clear polystyrene this time. It was pinned to a strip of wood shaped to the required contour and then gently and slowly softened with a miniature butane blow torch, keeping the torch on the move all the while.

203.

When sufficiently soft, the bulldog clip automatically pulls it down over the mould.

204.

Making these partitions, and those on the deck below, was one of the most time consuming and sometimes frustrating jobs on the whole project, particularly because much of the work becomes invisible on the final model. Once the basic structure is made, the remainder of the work is fairly straightforward but the initial job of cutting the transparent material to shape and ensuring a good fit to the bulwarks and deck can be trying, as is the task of ensuring that the top has the correct camber and will fit neatly beneath the deck above. It is also important to ensure that the partitions are vertical and I found it helpful to glue a small piece of wood to a square, to counter the sheer of the deck, to accurately check that the partitions were all truly vertical.

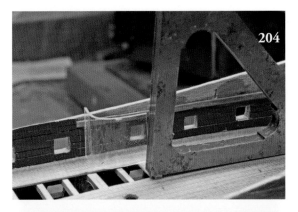

205.

The framework for the partitions. Note the different heights and notches cut for one of the poop deck beams.

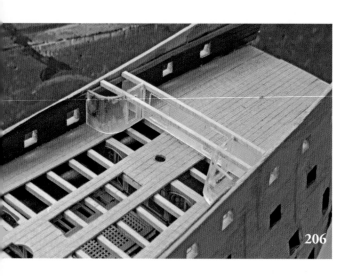

206

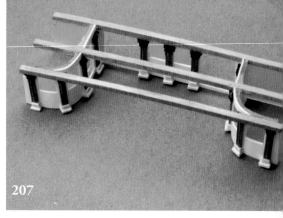

207

206.

With two of the beams glued in place the whole structure becomes far more rigid but can still be easily removed and replaced during detailing to repeatedly check for fit.

207.

The work proceeding in similar vein to the earlier partitions.

208

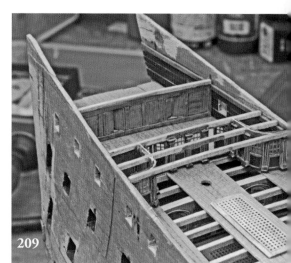

209

208.

Finished, stained and ready for installation on the model.

209.

The aftmost partition can be permanently glued to the hull, but before finally fitting the forward partition the gun ports must be be cleaned up and painted, ring bolts fitted for the guns and a wheel made.

210.

211.

The wheel during construction. I had the brass etched parts made to my specification some years ago now. Each wheel is formed from three parts, a central wheel plus spokes, sandwiched between two rims. They are glued together with Superglue and the spokes built up with white glue. The supports were made from box and the barrel turned in a drill chuck. Incidentally, I was subsequently dissatisfied with the barrel and remade it, slightly smaller and with a raised rim at either end. Before I had my brass etch, I used to make the rims from paper, firstly punching a disk and then removing its centre with a slightly smaller punch, while the spokes were made from wire, I doubt there would be any real difference in the appearance of the finished item, but the brass etch certainly makes the job easier. In the background can be seen blanks for wheels of various sizes.

The wheel has been completed and fitted, along with the remaining deck beams.

A chequered 'canvas' floor covering has been fitted in the captain's cabin, and this was printed on the computer. Before I had a computer, I used to draw and shade in an area of over-scale chequer, photocopy it numerous times, glue the pieces together, and then progressively reduce the size using a photocopier.

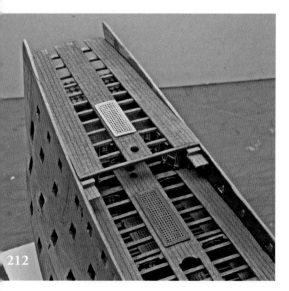

212.

I have fitted the deck planking and also a step and small platform that will lead, via a spiral staircase, to the quarterdeck below. The same has been done at the break of the forecastle and quarterdeck leading down to the upper deck. A scalpel was used to cut a shallow groove in the bulwarks into which the platform was glued. There is still the shelter to be fitted right aft on the poop but for reasons that will become apparent this is best left till later. It is now time to leave the remaining deck details and move on to the broadside planking.

213.

It is now time to bid a fond goodbye to the middle deck and glue the two sections of hull together. With an unrigged model such as this, however, much of the work down below will be glimpsed through the open gun ports and between the frames.

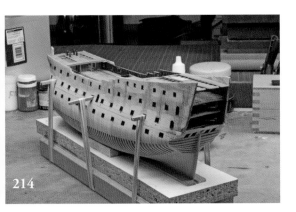

214.

215.

The assembled hull is put under tension using elastic bands as can be seen here; it is then possible to check carefully that the join is tight all the way around the hull before flooding it with very thin Superglue.

Now, working from the plans, and taking measurements from the bottom edge of the lower deck gun ports, the position of the lower wale is marked on the hull. A strip of masking tape slightly narrower than the wale is then cut and applied to the hull giving a good visual impression of its run. Both sides of the ship are taped before checking from all angles that the lines both look right and are correctly positioned. A pencil line is drawn either side of the tapes before they are removed.

216.

I prepared some holly for the main wales because it is a timber that I find takes a bend well. I have used heat from the shank of a soldering iron to pre-shape items such as these, but on this occasion made quite a set in the timbers

by bending and shaping by hand before fitting them to the hull. However, once they were in place, I took the precaution of dowelling them around both the bow and stern. This photograph shows the pre-painted upper timber being glued in place; a careful check needs to be kept on the distance from the lower ports.

217.

218.

After from the main wale was fitted, the remainder of the ship's side was planked with yellow cedar shavings. For the majority of the hull, these were mounted on paper but those used for the topsides were unmounted to help reduce the overall thickness of the upper deck bulwarks.

The shavings and hull were both treated with a generous coat of Seccotine that was allowed to dry thoroughly before trimming off the individual planks. When gluing these to the hull, a further coat of thin Seccotine was given to the back of each plank in turn.

One plank of yellow cedar has here been fitted below the upper wale timber before fitting the lower wale. The planking now proceeds upwards, with the ports being opened up after fitting each plank. Shorter lengths of plank can be fitted between ports where appropriate.

To cut the cedar planks to a uniform width, a straight edge, in this case an old white plastic rule, seen here upside down, has had a small block of plastic card glued to either end, the thickness of which represents the width of plank to be cut. The white rule is offered up to the edge of the planking material and then the steel straight edge slid across it until it is hard up against the plastic stops; the white rule is then moved away and the plank trimmed off with the knife.

219.

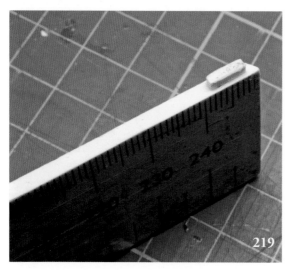

One of the blocks of plastic in close-up. If the planks are to be longer than a rule, this can easily be facilitated by trimming enough of the underside of the blocks away to allow the planking material to slide beneath them.

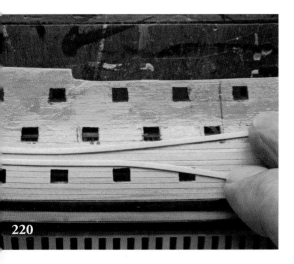

220.

The middle wale is being formed by laying two planks of mounted yellow cedar over the top of the existing planking. The planks running immediately beneath the wale timbers are cut narrower than the rest and the plank between the two timbers is wider. This ensures that when the wale is fitted any slight discrepancy with the run of the wale won't be disclosed by any exposed seams.

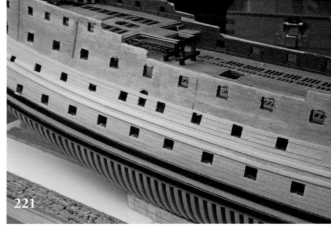

221.

The planking proceeding up the side of the ship.

222.

The remainder of the planking has been applied to the ship's side and the upper wale fitted in the same manner as the middle. Slots for the channels have been cut, initially with the Minicraft grinding wheel, before cleaning up with a small file.

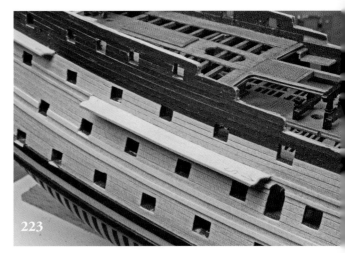

223.

The channels were cut from box and glued into their rebates.

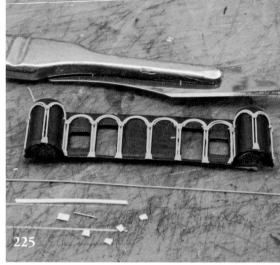

224.

The beakhead bulkhead is temporarily returned to the model and the roundhouses (cut from a convenient length of dowel) are glued to it along with the card skirting and uprights. To the fore are the knightheads and holes for these have been drilled either side of the bowsprit housing. The latter was drilled slightly undersize before being opened up with burrs.

225.

The bulkhead removed and further detailed, it was then put on one side for finishing and fitting at a later stage.

226.

It is now time attend to the little cabin at the aft of the poop deck (the coach). As you can see from the photograph, I have made a card template for the forward end and prepared a piece of boxwood from which the beams will be cut from.

227.

The drum sander is used to remove the surplus wood on the underside.

228.

The forward bulkhead has been prepared in the usual manner – a beam shelf fitted on either side and the beams cut and glued in place.

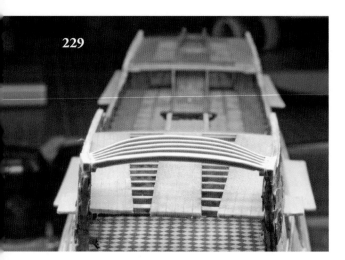

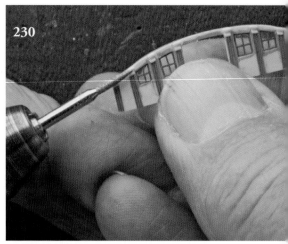

229.

The extreme and varying camber of these beams shows up well here, and can be further accentuated with a curved sanding block.

230.

Detailing the bulkhead.

231.

The stern galleries, which must now be tackled, represent a formidable challenge to even the most proficient of modellers. There are, as far as I am aware, no published works covering the building of a First Rate's stern of this period, and to make things even more difficult and confusing for this work, at any rate, is that the models of *Royal William* and

Royal George, the contemporary engraving, and the plans of the ship herself are at considerable variance one with another. The photograph shows grooves cut in the ships sides for the quarter gallery decks (these were cut with a Minicraft grinding wheel). The rather rough templates were constructed from card; they need to be a good fit in these grooves and should also but up tightly to the ends of their respective decks.

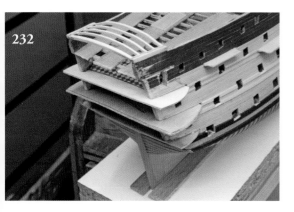

232.

1/32in-thick ply decks are cut and prepared from the templates.

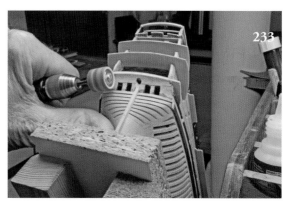

233.

A fillet of wood has been glued under the lower deck and is here being faired in to complete the upper counter.

234.

Another timber is now cut from the same sheet of ply; it will define the top of the upper counter and slots into notches cut into the hull and into little tenons at the fore end of the galleries.

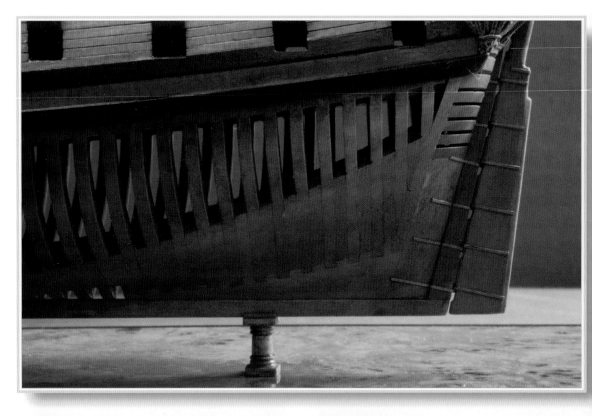

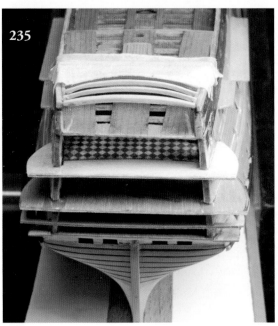

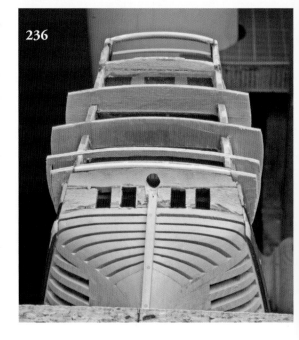

235 & 236.

The decks seen from above and below.

237.

Templates being prepared for the stern bulkheads. The uprights at both sides were fitted first so that the templates could be located against them; one is visible just to the left of the template held in the tweezers. The holes allow tweezers to be used as handles.

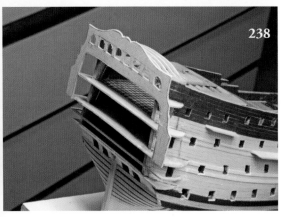

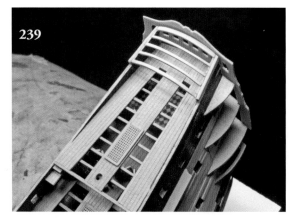

238 & 239.

Rebates have been cut in the aft corners of the decks to accept the stern timber which has been

temporarily fixed to check for all round fit. I cut this to shape using the plans of the ship but I found it required redefining later on.

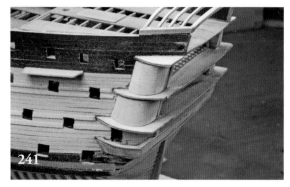

240.

There are many ways of building up the galleries, but on this model I used blocks of jelutong that were roughly cut as shown to fit between the decks and flush to the side of the ship.

241.

They were then removed to be finished and shaped. Note that the blocks encompass the glazed areas as well.

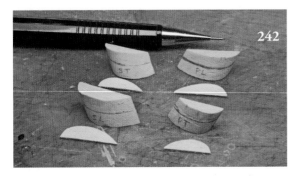

242.

The blocks were removed again, and the extent of the glazed area marked and a sliver of timber taken from the top of each.

243.

Now the top section of each block can be removed and discarded and the lower section hollowed out using appropriate burrs. Each one is then faced with thin card and glued in place on the model along with the thin sections cut from the top of the original blocks; these are fitted beneath the deck above.

244.

The upper counter has been filled in with a strip of jellutong. This has been extended around the galleries, shaping the blocks in the same manner as used for those above.

The glazing, cut from strips of suitable acetate, can now be fitted. I find a good contact adhesive best for this job; Superglue must be avoided because if it

makes its way inside the hull at any point, even in very small quantities, the fumes can cloud the acetate. Incidentally, it is worth collecting samples of acetate from packaging for these sorts of application.

245.

The horizontal glazing bars can be fitted in continuous lengths.

246.

The rounded arches for the tops of the windows punched out and trimmed to size.

247.

The uprights and vertical glazing bars are then fitted and followed by the arches.

248.

The same process is now carried round the side of the galleries and the panelling beneath the windows built up with card.

249.

Columns are the next feature to be added and are constructed in the same way as those on the interior partitions.

250.

The middle deck stern winows. Note the unfinished brackets beneath the upper deck stern walk and the short lengths of polystyrene rod used to embellish both ends of the columns.

251.

Boxing in the sides of the hull.

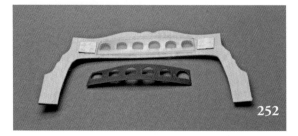

252.

Before fitting the stern, the inboard side is fitted with acetate followed by red painted paper lining; this is traced from the stern and carefully trimmed out with a scalpel. The windows on both sides of the hull can be fitted as dummies so they have been papered over with gloss black painted paper.

253.

Turn over stern and add the detailing to the windows.

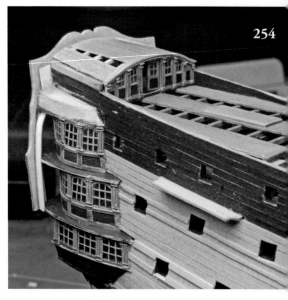

254.

The stern now glued in place on the model. The forward bulkhead of the coach and the planking on the deck over the top are added as well.

255.

The handrails around the galleries are located in tenons cut through the planking at their forward end and slotted onto the strip of card glued to the stern. The upper unfinished rail is temporarily propped in place.

256.

The rails sanded down.

257.

Before fitting them permanently, lengths of wire are glued to the inboard underside faces of the rails. The rail closest to the camera is for the stern walk. Note also that wires have been glued to the decks just inboard of their edges.

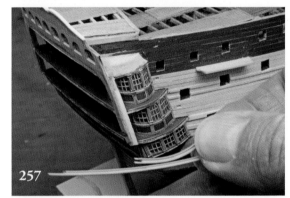

258.

A strip of card has been fitted to form the top edge of the coving over the upper stern walk and I have used some more to raise the level of the stern. I used Superglue for this job and then flooded the card with some super thin Superglue, which, when dry, renders the card very amenable to sanding and grinding to a smooth finish.

259.

The underside of the coving has been filled and is now being sanded down. I decided I had not made the card strip wide enough so added a rolled out length of epoxy modelling putty, which explains the green colour. Note how it has been faired in at the ends.

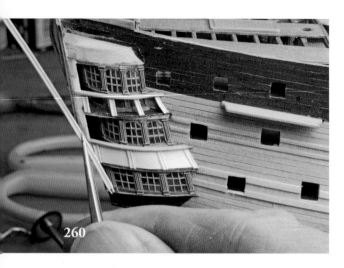

260.

To build up the side, take a strip of very thin card, held in tweezers, which has two card beads glued either side. Sections can be cut from it and be fitted as shown to the wire supports beneath the rails and on the decks.

261.

The wire balusters fitted.

262.

The same process is here applied to the stern and the rails are being built up with lengths of pre-painted wire.

263.

When fitting the rail around the top gallery, I found it easier to drill through the stern and drill a shallow hole for the forward end to locate in. Then the wire can be passed from the stern before gluing.

264.

After fitting the balusters, I added another wire to the outside and flooded the intervening space with superglue as shown.

265.

When dry, the rail is finished off with a coat of wood glue which can be sanded when hard. Rails formed from wire have been added.

266.

Paper borders are added to the panels round the lower gallery.

267.

The lower finishing can be carved from timber or, as here, built up with Milliput and then, when dry, finished with files and sandpaper.

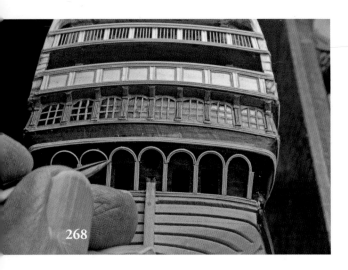

268.

The construction work on the stern is now just about finished. The final detail to the lower counter is being added, the hoops of wire being wound like a tight spring on a suitably sized rod before cutting to size.

269.

With the framework of the stern in place it is time to move on to the head and broadsides of the model to bring them to a similar degree of finish. Protection for the delicate stern structure has been added using a few roughly cut scraps of ply, Superglue and tape.

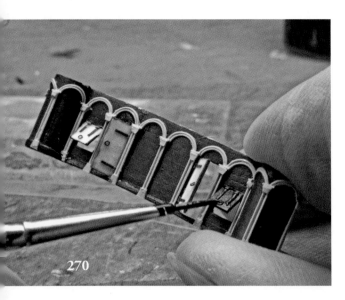

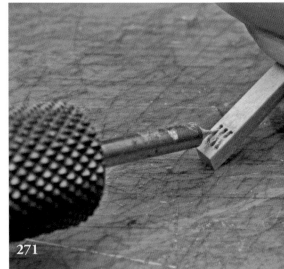

270.

After making, fitting and painting doors and gun port lids, the beakhead partition can be finally glued in place.

271.

Next are the catheads which were made from boxwood, the sheaves first being drilled right through before being shaped as shown in the photograph with the home-made three-sided drill bit.

272.

The cathead glued to the deck. It is formed from two pieces of timber and the larger one dowelled down into the side of the ship. Protruding details are extremely vulnerable and need to be given a little extra strength. Note the beakhead partition and one of the two roundhouses. These were cut from scrap dowel and the moldings on the bulkhead continued around them.

273.

Next to be fitted are the cheeks and bolsters, both of which were shaped using boiling water and the soldering iron shank.

274.

Bolsters and cheeks fitted and the cheeks being subsequently further refined with the drum sander.

275.

One of the main rails being formed from 1mm ply. I took the shape from the plans but juggled the dimensions to compensate for the perspective view which was obviously shown there.

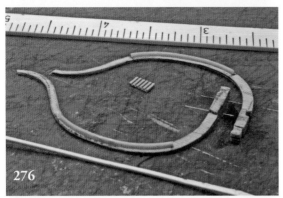

276.

Having cut the main rails from the ply, the heads are squared up with a layer of box glued either side before shaping the tops with a small file. On the inside faces card shelves for the gratings have been glued. These should be set the thickness of a grating from the top of the rail

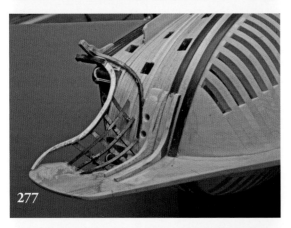

277.

With the top rails fitted I have moved on to the head timbers and the remaining rails. I have once again used some thin card, which, when I was satisfied with their positions and their run viewed from all angles, were again flooded with penetrating super glue.

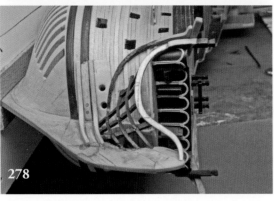

278.

The next stage is to cut and fit pieces of card between the rails to thicken the head timbers. The photo is the right way round; I find this work is best carried out with the model mounted on its side.

279.

This is followed by gluing wire to the rails to represent the mouldings. If you look carefully at the far ends of the middle rails, it is possible to just see that holes were drilled in the hull to take the ends of the wires. This makes it a lot easier to start the gluing process.

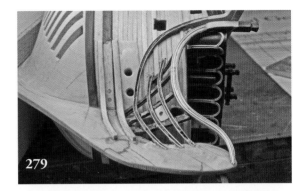

281.

280.

Strips of paper are now glued over the head timbers and over the top of the wire on the rails

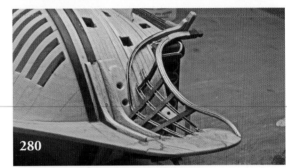

281.

The head timbers and rails have been well soaked with Superglue and any tidying up required can be done with burr and file. They have been given a coat of paint and are here having the relief decoration built up with artist's gesso, applied with a fine sable.

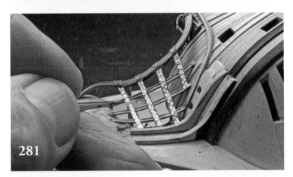

282.

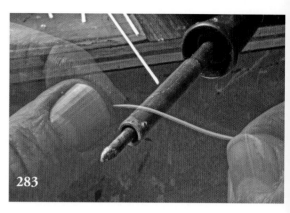

283.

282.

With the main structure of the head in place we should turn our attention to the broadsides. It is important to get at least on coat of stain on the planking before fitting the gratings over the head, which renders the area beneath somewhat inaccessible. The first item to be fitted is the anchor lining. On the ship itself they would be formed from separate planks of wood but on the majority of Navy Board models they seem to be made of single sheets of timber, which is how I have chosen to show them here. They were cut from mounted yellow cedar shavings and the mouldings at the sides scored with a knife.

283.

The chesstrees and fenders were cut from box and shaped as shown over a soldering iron shank. A little experimentation will pay off here; if the iron is too hot the wood will burn and become brittle, too cool and the wood won't take a curve. It is also necessary, with shallow curves such as these, to keep the wood on the move, backwards and forwards across the iron all the while its being shaped.

284.

285.

284.

The positions for the chesstrees and fenders being marked on the broadsides.

A piece of card cut with an accurate right angle is being used to ensure that they are all parallel and vertical.

285.

Rather than try and cut rebates in the fenders to fit over the wales, the easier option is to trim gaps in the wales into which the fenders can be glued.

286.

Next to be fitted are the channel knees. These need to be cut to fit tightly between the top of the channel and the side of the ship. The curved edge need only be cut roughly to shape at this stage, if at all.

287 & 288.

After gluing the knees in place they can be shaped, first with a drum sander before finishing the job with a fine diamond burr.

289.

The tops of the entrance ports and also the top of the belfry are frequently of a distinctive cruciform design, though not always so. There are many variations here as with other features on these models, but for *Royal George* I am sticking to the cruciform design. The first requirement is some half round material that can be made up from wood shavings or plastic card or rod, if any can be found of the right diameter. The photo shows some card being teased to shape around a length of dowel.

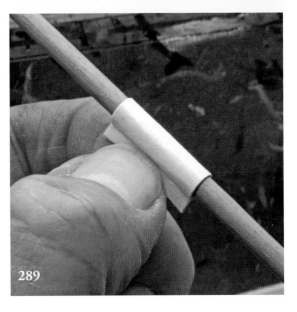

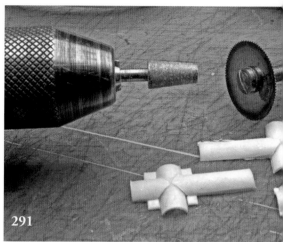

290.

The card tube is now held in a plastic clamp and soaked with liquid Superglue.

291.

The tube can then be trimmed as shown, first cut in half lengthways and then cut or sanded to a 90 degree point.

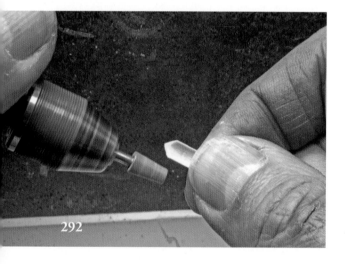

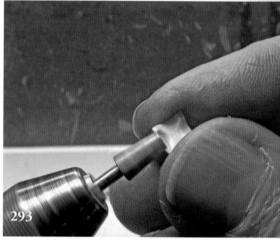

292.

The sections of card are then trimmed and assembled as shown here.

293.

They can then be cleaned up with the diamond burr both above and below the canopy.

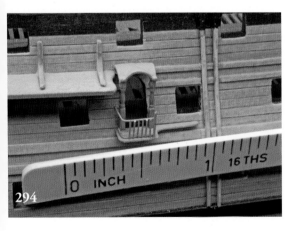

294.

The first canopy fitted to the model. The base for the entrance port was cut from box, the two pillars turned in the drill chuck, and the railings are being applied to the two lengths of wire at top and bottom. Note also the fenders fitted in the gaps trimmed in the wales.

295.

The port canopy, the rail has been completed as shown in photogtaphs 264 and 265. The steps for the ladder up the ship's side were cut from box, each being made up in two parts: a thin strip for the step and a small square one fitted beneath to form the supporting moulding. Both need some shaping and sanding before and after fitting.

296.

Now to tackle those somewhat daunting spiral stairs. Each step is formed from a rectangle of wood. They are glued together fanning out from a common axis at the front corner of each step. The trick here is to check carefully the thickness of the timber to ensure the correct number of steps fitting between the various decks and to spread the fan, step by step, just the right amount so that you end up with the requisite number of steps when the top step is set exactly 90 degrees from the bottom step. I have no method to pass on for this procedure; it is just trial and error.

297.

Three of the assembled spiral stairs. On the left is a flight that has not yet been cut down to size, though it has been marked with pencil ready for sanding down. For this I would use a coarse sanding disk in a Minicraft drill. On the right is a flight that has been sanded down to its finished size, and in the centre is a finished stair, the underside of which has been cut back to a smooth finish with a small sanding drum.

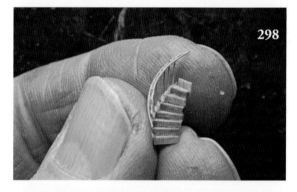

298.

A narrow strip of card was cut and glued around the outside curve of the stairs to form the base rail, which was drilled to accept the balusters. These were cut from wire and the rail built up in the same way as the rail around the entry ports.

299.

300.

There are various small windows in evidence on the broadside aft. The exact positioning and number of these vary from model to model and from the plans to the engraving. I have gone along with the plans for my layout. I omitted to provide openings for these at an earlier stage when it would have been practical to have done so, so have backed them with some cellophane painted a dark grey on the reverse side.

The upper or topgallant rails being fitted. Box was used for this, except for the curved sections marking the transition from one level to another. For these I used strips of ABS plastic. There is no need to pre-heat it in order to form the curve; it can just be bent to shape and will hold its curve.

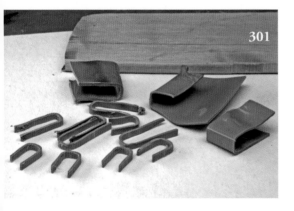

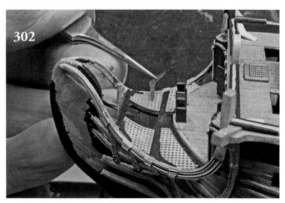

301.

302.

On both the *Royal George* plans and on the *Royal William* full hull model there is an archway in the centre of the rail over the beakhead bulkhead. The plans and the engraving also show four arched gun ports either side of the forecastle. I formed these, once again, from ABS plastic, this time softening the plastic with the blow torch (see photograph 202) before pulling it over the wooden former. A few burnt fingers later I was left with the shaped sections shown in the photo. These were then trimmed down before slicing off the individual arches on the Preac saw.

The arch over the beakhead bulkhead is now in place and a solid bulwark and capping rail fitted either side of it. Two head beams now connect the two main rails and central carlings connect these fore and aft. They are all fitted with ledges similar to those fitted to the main rails to support the gratings (see photograph 276) and the gratings have been cut to shape and glued to these ledges. The knightheads have been added to the model and here knees are being fitted between the beams and rails. Cutting them from paper ensures a very neat finish.

303.

Now the false rail is being glued in place and I am again using thin card, which after fitting will be treated once again with Superglue. Working with card in this way makes it very easy to follow complex curves; the alternative is to shape the rail from wood, something I have done many times in the past. The extra shaping to the top of the rail was added afterwards in the form of shallow card wedges. These were finally faired in and finished with a diamond burr.

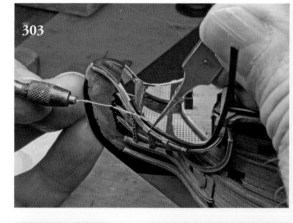

304.

The seats of ease have been fabricated from mounted wood shavings and I am in the process of building up the decorative moulding along the top of the bulkhead. In the tweezers is one of the balusters being fitted to the rail around the top of the roundhouse.

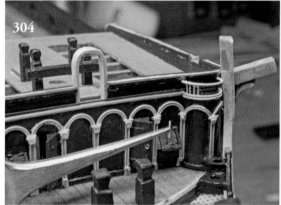

305.

Using a very fine brush, glue and then paint is being used to build up the centers of the balusters.

306.

Now, turning our attention inboard, to the waist of the ship, you will see that I have fitted the stairs, though one of the balusters needs replacing and there is still finishing work to do on them. This photograph shows the process of constructing the rails around the break of the quarterdeck. Because of their shape I used 0.5mm ply for strength. Two will be required each side – an upper and lower. They are first of all cut roughly to size before fixing them together in pairs with narrow strips of double-sided tape. They are then given a further sand down to ensure that upper and lower rails are identical. Each pair is then fixed to the deck with more double-sided tape and the positions of the uprights marked and drilled through both the rails and the deck.

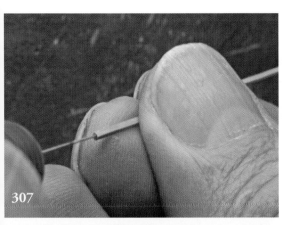

307.

I am making the uprights square beneath the lower rail and round above, built up to the desired shape with glue. They will be formed around a wire that will pass through the square base and both rails. The square bases were formed from box. I drilled the end of a strip as shown here.

308.

With a strip of wood fitted to the saw guide for support, individual sections were carefully cut off. After each cut the end of the strip was drilled a little further.

309.

The square sections can now be glued onto their wires, painted and left to dry.

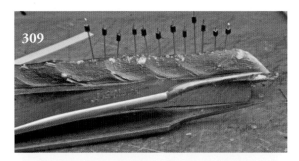

310.

The rails being assembled. All that remains to be done is to cut and sand the wires flush with the tops of the rails and build up the uprights with glue

311.

312.

The next fitting to be dealt with is the belfry. Four identical pillars are required. One is here being turned in the drill chuck using a jeweller's file.

The bell was also turned in the drill chuck, first with the sanding disk for rough shaping before finishing the job with a file and some very fine wet and dry paper. A fine tail should be left on the top of the bell for attaching it to the bell beam.

313.

314.

The completed belfry. The canopy was finished earlier (photographs 289–293) so the only detail that requires further explanation is the wheel and I made this from one of my brass etchings (photograph 110) but it would be a very straightforward job to make from wire.

One other detail that needs adding to this area of the deck is a handrail from the top of the stairs to the quarterdeck. I made this from a strip of box with a length of wire glued on top. Also note that the tops of the stair posts have been sanded level and glass beads glued on their tops.

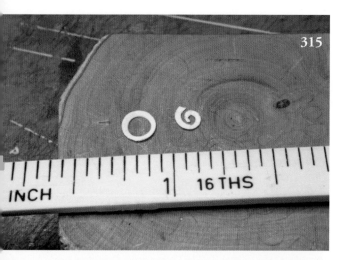

315.

Moving outboard once again I am tackling the decorative mouldings. These will be represented with strips of pre-painted tissue paper and wire. The scrolls at the ends of these mouldings were punched from paper, trimmed, moistened, shaped as shown, pressed flat and allowed to dry thoroughly before painting.

316.

Scrolls in place and the tissue strips being applied to the hull.

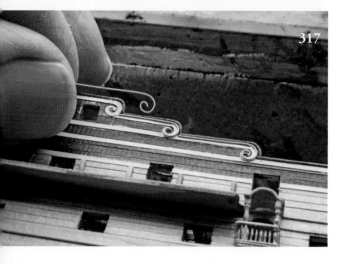

317.

The wires shaped and being applied. I am reminded at this point, and at many others throughout this book, that close-up photographs under harsh light do little to flatter; they show up blemishes that will become invisible to the naked eye.

᏶ *Carving and Decoration* ᏶

One of the most enjoyable, but also possibly the most challenging, task encountered on a model of this period is making the wealth of carving and decoration. I actually find it a relief, a holiday if you like, from the more exacting process of hull construction. I can't give a definitive guide to how to go about this work because I approach it differently with each model. However, I usually follow the techniques shown here, or some of them anyway, depending of course on the complexity of the job in hand. As the work progressed I jumped back and forth from figurehead to stern, with attention to the broadsides sandwiched somewhere in between, and I have kept the sequence of the photographs in that order, as to progress in this way seemed logical at the time with similar stages of the work being completed, to some extent at least, in tandem. I must stress here that these are simply the solutions that came to mind as I worked and I leave you to be the judge of their success.

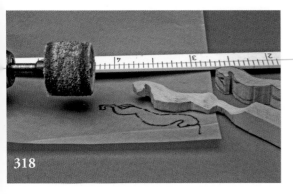

318

319

318.

The first feature to be tackled is the equestrian figurehead. This was a first for me and a daunting undertaking. I found it a great help to take some of the photographs of the figureheads of *Royal George* and *Royal William,* import them into a Word folder and reduce them to the scale of the model. I was then able to take dimensions directly from them. A tracing was taken from the drawing I had added to the plans (photograph 101), transferred to a suitably sized strip of box and roughly shaped with the drum sander as shown here.

319.

The two horses have been worked on with a variety of diamond burrs to a reasonable degree of finish and glued to the bow. A wire armature for the rider has been made and glued on the horse's back ready for building up with gesso, one of the possible methods for constructing miniature figures. In retrospect, I would not have built the figurehead up in quite this way if I were doing the job again but would have made the whole structure removable from the stem until it was finished.

320.

Holes have been drilled and wires glued in them from which the forelegs are being formed and a bunch of fine wires are being used to form a tail.

320

321.

322.

Moving back to the stern, I am treating the figures to be found there in the same manner. I decided to experiment with various woods hoping to find something softer that would allow me to be a little more expressive and free when working with the burrs. King George's bust was carved from jelutong, which was acceptable though a bit grainy. I then tried some tupelo. I have used this for carving seas in the past and it is horrendous to work with unless your tools are absolutely razor sharp. I found it sanded easily and very quickly with both sander and burrs and took an excellent finish and, as can be seen here, it has no discernable grain and it seems to work equally well when sanded or cut in any direction.

Some of the roughly carved figures have been fitted in place at the stern. The blobs between the windows will be cherubs' heads. The green material that is being used to build up the pillars and covings is an epoxy putty with the apt name of Green Stuff. I prepared and rolled out some sheets of this some years ago; when set it remains very flexible, easily cut, rather like hard cheese. I find it useful when clean curves like these are required, and it sands to a good finish.

323.

The main figures have been rather roughly carved and mounted on the stern and where applicable wire armatures for arms and legs fitted.

324.

I experimented with tissue paper for some of the figures' clothing on this model, and was pleased with the results. When applying them, the strips are moistened before anchoring one end to the figure. This leaves you free to twist and shape the remainder until satisfied. When dry it is treated with thin Superglue.

325.

With the main framework of figures and their drapes and clothes established, the remaining decoration can be built up, in gradual layers, using gesso.

326.

There are decorative friezes along the broadside that also need to be built up in low relief. The first stage is to mark these in with white ink and a mapping pen. They are then built up with several applications of gesso using the finest of sable brushes. The decoration round the quarter gallery berthing (bottom right-hand corner of the picture) has already been built up in this way.

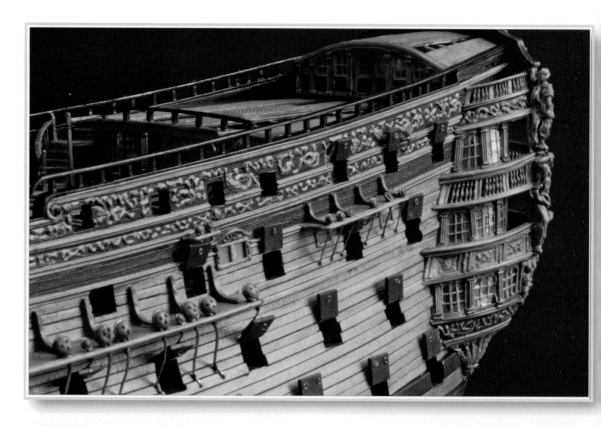

327.

A close-up shot of the quarter gallery berthing, showing the relief carving and below it a fan of paper strips radiating upwards around the drop. These will, in turn, be decorated with gesso, built up in the same manner.

328.

You may have noticed in some of the preceding photographs a clear plastic cover over the central section of the model. It is not only a precaution against accidental damage but also allows the model to be placed on the bench upside down while working on some of the areas of the bow and stern, and it is also useful when used as shown. It was made from scraps of polystyrene sheet, cobbled together with plumber's pipe weld.

329

330

329.

330.

Returning to the figurehead, the same treatment as used astern to build up the detail is used here. The tweezers are gripping the front section of the rider's corselet; this was cut from paper and the half round scallops punched from behind using the shank end of a drill bit. It is being glued in place. The figure is wearing a kilt of tissue paper.

A little further on with the work.

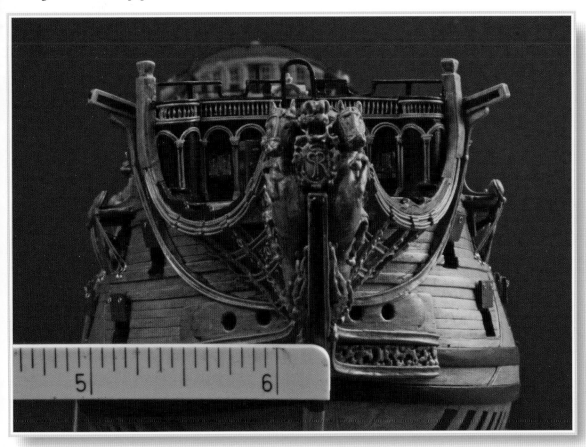

331.

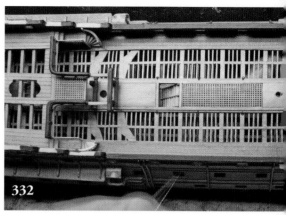

332.

331.

At this stage, I broke off to give the outside of the hull a couple more coats of varnish. The final finish needs to be attained prior to fitting port lids or deadeyes. Before applying any paint or varnish to any model, it is, of course, common sense to thoroughly dust everything. The outside of the model presents no problem, but the lower decks are not so easy. I solve this by using this brush. A few lengths of ordinary white string are trapped in the fold of a length of wire and the shank then wound tight in a drill chuck.

332.

The brush can be inserted through stern or side ports and twirled between finger and thumb. This needs to be accompanied by some vigorous blowing or, even better, a dust extractor or vacuum cleaner nozzle.

333.

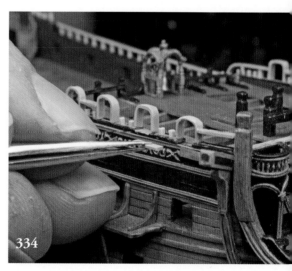

334.

333.

With a couple more coats of varnish on the outside of the hull, I am turning my attention to the rail that extends almost all of the way around the ship. I decided, for ease of construction and strength, to use ABS once again. The first job is marking and then drilling for the uprights. The round drill holes can then be punched square with this homemade punch ground from the end of a 4in nail. Some square section plastic was cut from sheet and short sections superglued into the holes.

334.

The rail in the process of being completed. All of the plastic to plastic joins are made with plastic-weld. The arches for the forecastle guns were made earlier (photograph 301).

335.

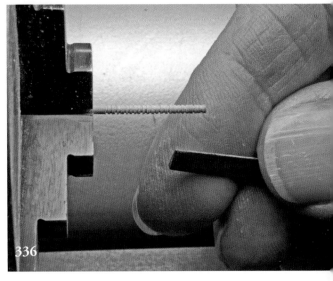

336.

The deadeyes were turned on the lathe, a job that could equally be carried out using a drill chuck, with the drill suitably mounted on a bench. I prepared a strip of boxwood rod and grooved it at regular intervals, and then alternate grooves were further defined using the razor saw.

For the smaller deadeyes the rod was so thin that turning was not an option, so the work was initially done with a fine file.

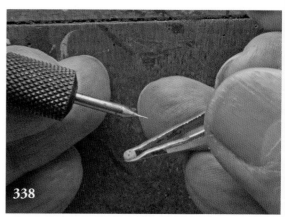

337.

Finally, strips of half a dozen or so deadeyes are placed in the drill chuck and further shaped with the fine file before parting them off with a sharp knife.

338.

I have an old pair of tweezers that have been bent and then ground to the shape shown here. They are invaluable for holding blocks and deadeyes while sanding or filing them to shape or, as here, drilling the lanyard holes.

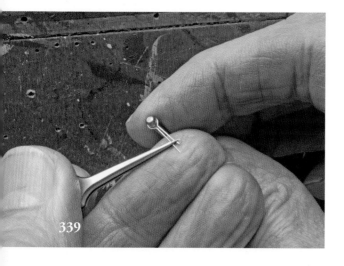

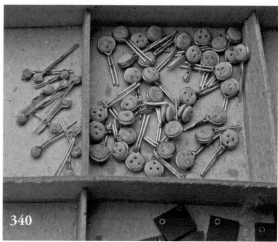

339.

Deadeye strops being formed from copper wire round a drill shank. They can then be painted with some gold or brass paint.

340.

Here the deadeyes are in their strops which are fitted with a small whipping of fine wire.

341.

341.

After giving the deadeyes a coat of varnish, grooves to accept them are cut in the channels and they are then glued in place.

342.

A strip of box was next prepared for the capping rail. This was cut to a square section on the Preac saw and shaped to a half round with my multitool made from a scrap of junior hacksaw blade. The various profiles cut in it were made with fine diamond burrs. In use it is repeatedly drawn along the piece of timber as shown here.

342.

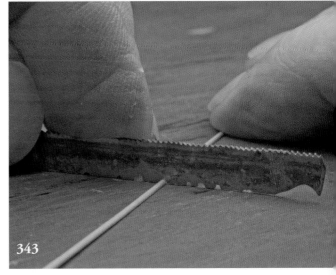

343.

343.

A capping rail fitted to its channel. A fine burr can then be used to trim the ends of the strops to just a small tail, sufficient to glue the top of the chain plates to. These were cut from paper strips soaked in Superglue. When fitted they were given a second coat using the wire applicator while the fixing bolts were suggested with white glue. They were finally given a coat of gold paint.

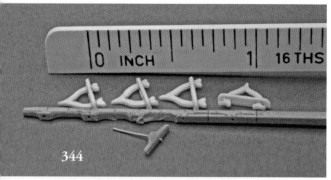

344.

Other fittings that have been left until this late stage are the cleats fitted in the waist of the ship and the staghorn kevels for the quarterdeck. Their construction is quite straightforward. I used plastic card for the kevels and box for the cleats.

345.

The port lids were cut from a strip of boxwood cut to the correct depth and thickness. This was then painted red on one side and varnished on the other; when dry the individual lids were sliced off on the Preac saw. They were then drilled for the ring bolts. As the lids were to be shown fully open the hinges were not fitted to their backs and only the rings on the undersides shown. These were made by winding pre-painted copper wire around a drill shank before separating the coils into individual rings with a sharp scalpel. Some fine lengths of wire were then bent sharply in the middle (right foreground). One of the rings was then threaded on each of these (left foreground) and both ends of each of these threaded through one of the holes in the lids. A spot of Superglue was then applied before cutting the remainder off with a sharp scalpel.

346.

The port lids were glued in place with a spot of Superglue, not a very reliable fixing, particularly between two varnished surfaces, so I then pinned them to the hull as shown in this photograph; I used copper wire dipped in Superglue. The wire was subsequently cut flush with the lid using a knife and was then finally finished with a diamond burr.

The work on the model is now really finished apart from touching up the varnish and paintwork until satisfied with the finish, or as satisfied as any of us ever can be with our own work.

∽*Making the Case* ∽

Miniature models are delicate and vulnerable objects and must be protected against dust and damage by a glass case; and having spent many, many hours building a model, it seems a shame not to dignify it with a case and plinth which shows it off to its advantage. There are of course many ways of accomplishing this but I have used the following method for many years.

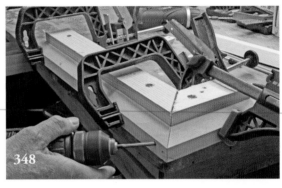

347.

The first job is to make up some suitable moulding for the base; I cut my own from some well-seasoned jelutong stock. In this photograph a rectangular sectioned billet is being passed under the angled blade to produce the desired section. The saw can then be returned to the vertical and lowered until just 10mm above the table and a rebate cut for the base board.

348.

I used to cut my own mitres on the table saw but I now get them cut by a local picture framer. He does a much better job. I have made up a very simple jig for the next stage of the work. It consists of a flat piece of board to which I have screwed two lengths of 2in x 2in. Two pieces of the framing are then clamped as shown and two holes, the same size as some dowel rod, drilled at an angle across the corner with care being taken not to break right through to the outside of the other piece.

349.

Small and shallow plugs of jelutong are now prepared. Strips were cut across the grain, rounded up with chisel and sanding disk before cutting and inserting as shown. They can then be glued in place with a touch of Superglue. When this has dried a sharp chisel is used to trim them level with the base.

350.

This leaves us with four sides with perfectly aligned hidden holes which, when fitted with the dowels, will ensure a strong and accurate join. Also clearly seen here is the rebate for the baseboard.

351.

Four matched sheets of oak burr veneer that have been chosen for this case. The first job is to take the bumps and cockles out of it, at least to some extent, so making it much easier to work with and glue. This is accomplished by soaking the veneer for a minute or two in very hot water before layering it between sheets of chipboard to dry. The four sections are selected so that the design radiates as identically as possible from the centre, and the four sides are prepared so that identical patterns extend outwards from the centre. Cutting the veneer from the four sheets allows both sides to be identical and both ends the same. Here the sheets have been cut and joined as tightly as possible with strips of masking tape.

352.

Now they are turned over and joined on the other side with strips of gummed tape in the sequence and manner shown in this photograph. The tape should be the brown paper variety that needs licking or moistening before use. The veneer should once again be placed between the sheets of chipboard to keep them flat whilst drying. As the tape dries out it will tend to shrink slightly, pulling the edges even closer together.

353.

My favoured glue for veneering is the product that goes by the name of Gluefilm. In appearance it is rather like large sheets of double sided tape but the adhesive layer only melts when heat is applied. In use, a suitably sized sheet is ironed on to the backing surface and the veneer ironed in place while working it down with either a veneer hammer or a block of wood. The oak burr veneer I used proved positively evil to lay, and I would recommend something easier if you are coming to this task for the first time. To counter the problem of adhesion, I applied a layer of the Gluefilm to the back of the veneer as well.

354 & 355.

When this has been done the backing is peeled away and the two surfaces brought together and glued to the case with an iron and a veneer hammer. The front of each side is veneered first; then when cool the veneer is trimmed flush top and bottom.

356.

Now the front of each side is treated in the same manner. The strip of wood that the case side is resting on forms a cradle for the work piece and gives a horizontal surface to work on. Here it has been temporarily fixed to the bench with double-sided tape to give some stability. I have several of these strips; they can also be used when applying veneer with white glue, allowing a batten to be placed on top of the veneer and clamped while the glue dries.

357.

All the edges of the veneer can now be cleaned up with knife, chisel and sanding block. Particular care should be extended to the mitred ends, which should be finished with a sharp chisel as shown here.

358.

When satisfied that the joins are as perfect as I can get them, the four sides and the dowels are glued, reassembled and clamped.

359.

After leaving to thoroughly dry, the clamps are removed, the base turned over and a ply or fibreboard base cut to fit the recess and glued in place.

360.

I usually use lime or jellutong for the plinths, but I was out of both of suitable dimensions so used a piece of tupelo instead. Anything stable would do and I see no reason why fibreboard would not serve just as well. Here, I am gluing down the four matching quarters of veneer last seen in photographs 351 and 352.

361.

The edge of the veneer is then scored all round the edge to allow for the fitting of a border and the surplus carefully removed with a knife.

362.

I used black veneer for the border. The sides are first of all fitted followed by the narrow band around the top.

363.

When gluing these strips down I did not go all the way to the ends with the iron, but they were left to overlap as shown. The mitres were then cut in one stroke and the ends ironed and pressed firmly down and together.

364

365

364.

With a difficult veneer such as the oak burr, it helps to start the finishing work with either a cabinet maker's scraper or, as here, a piece of glass.

365.

There has always been something of a mystique about glass cutting, but I do assure you it is quite unwarranted and, with a little practice, anyone can learn to do it. The secret is to buy from a glass dealer a really good cutter, which will last for many years. When using it only press hard enough to lightly score the surface of the glass, which should make a silky swishing sound, not a grinding splintering sound; the latter sound indicates that you are pressing too hard. Then, as if by magic, the glass will break cleanly straight along the line of the score.

When cutting glass for a case such as this, accuracy is essential and that is why it is best to cut your own. I carefully measure for each cut, mark the glass with a very fine black fibre-tip pen, and then make sure that the wheel of the cutter runs exactly through the centre of the marks before finally making the cut.

I have tried various methods for gluing glass together, from silicone to Glass Bond. This latter is a cyanoacrylic, and is finally set off by exposure to ultraviolet light. This means that the cover can be assembled with the glue fluid unset and taped together in artificial light before being taken on a board to the windowsill where it will set almost immediately in a good light. The real disadvantage is the eventuality of having to disassemble the cover or replace a scratched or damaged pane, which is almost impossible. Recently, I have been using Evo-Stik impact adhesive, which I have found it to be as good as any other, and was used for this case.

First, the four sides are cut and holes drilled with a diamond burr near the bottom of the end panes; these are for the final fixing down of the cover. Then I like to remove the sharp edges of the glass with a sharpening stone before giving them all a good wash and rinse. The four sides are then assembled with Evo-Stik and when set carefully positioned in the base as in the photograph. When satisfied that they are sitting square within the base, the top pane is carefully marked, cut and glued to the sides. Next, gumstrip is glued around all the edges adhesive side down, again using the Evo-Stik. This binds the panes together and provides the surface to which the veneer edging is glued.

366.

Now, using a straight edge and craft knife, strips of veneer are prepared. Sixteen lengths are required, eight of which should be slightly wider than the others as these will cover the edges of the first strips fitted. In this photograph, the first (narrow) strip is being glued to the top of the case. The wide gumstrip has been fitted and the Evo-Stik used to coat both this and the underside of the veneer. A small square of non-stick paper has been placed over the corner and a larger piece laid along the remainder of the side, leaving just half an inch or so of the gumstrip exposed. The veneer strip is being laid in place over these with the aid of a strip of card, used to ensure that the veneer lines up exactly with the edge of the case. Once this section has been pressed down the large piece of paper can be withdrawn a little further and the process repeated. When the far end of the case is reached, another small square of non-stick paper is inserted beneath the veneer.

367.

When two edges have been fitted, the mitre is cut with a knife as shown here; the paper square can then be withdrawn and the veneer bedded down.

368.

Once all the veneer edges have been fitted, I like to mask the glass before starting to rub down all the veneer surfaces. If you have been examining the photographs carefully you may have noticed some damage to the veneer in places; this was unavoidable with such a brittle and difficult burr. So, before moving on, repairs were made with scraps of the original veneer. Small blemishes were repaired with proprietary filler. I have resolved to invest in a glue pot and some scotch glue before embarking on the next case using burr veneer. Being applied wet and hot it softens the veneer while laying and this helps prevent the shrinkage that can occur when using Gluefilm. I would advise anyone planning to work with burr veneers to experiment with different glues before making a start on a case.

Once brought to a good finish, the case and plinth were given at least a dozen coats of polyurethane varnish, rubbing down lightly several times during the process. It was then finally rubbed down and levelled using some 600 grit wet-and-dry paper before polishing with automobile cutting compound and metal polish.

369.

The plinth needs to be screwed to the base, but before doing so needs to be accurately centred. I find an easy way of doing this is by jamming pieces of card between them, obviously using the exact same number and thickness of pieces at each location; two along each side and one at either end.

370.

Now the base is turned over and four holes drilled, countersunk, and screws inserted. The photograph also shows one of the recesses ground at either end of the case for tying down the glass cover. The screws can now be removed and replaced at will, the plinth always returning to its central position.

371.

Holes have been drilled through the base for the wire or twine used to tie down the cover. In practice the wire is passed through the hole in the glass and then both ends passed down through the base before tying them around a short length of brass or steel rod, part of a panel pin is fine. When all of this work has been done, the plinth is removed and the base and inside are given several coats of dark grey paint. I shall then, before finally assembling the case, fit a strip of foam draught excluder around the inside edge of the base for the glass to bed down on. With the glass fitted the recesses for the brass rod can then be filled in with plasticine or some other easily removable modelling putty and a rectangle of self adhesive green baize applied to the base.

372.

The supporting pillars for the model were turned on the unimat, the main features formed with the home-shaped fine turning tool to be seen in the tool holder. They were then finished off with very fine needle files and sand paper.

373 & 374.

They are then parted off from one another and individually drilled with a bit in the tailstock to accept the screwed rod before fitting the strips of boxwood quadrant, sanding the tops and bases to a square section and finally cleaning up and varnishing.

375.

Two final items are the brass supports fitted either side of the hull. They were initially turned in a drill chuck with sanding disks and files, and then the ends beaten flat before finishing the shaping with a fine file, and then wet-and-dry and metal polish. They were drilled for the tiny brass pins, of the type used for fitting model railway track, and they also were turned in the drill chuck to reduce their dimension a little before cutting them short and re-sharpening the points.

This brings me nearly to the end of yet another model. Brass plates for the case have to be ordered, and then the whole ensemble is finished. This miniature Navy Board model was a fascinating, demanding and very rewarding project that took some 1,500 hours, spread over 16 months, to complete. Much of this was quite intensive, and perhaps not feasible for many amateur modellers, but I hope that any model shipwright will have found in these pages something new, something to take on to the next model that he builds.

ᗞ *Model Gallery* ᗞ

Centurion 1732

Centurion is well known as the ship commanded by Captain George Anson on his famous circumnavigation. She set out in 1740 and was the only ship to survive the voyage, finally returning home in June 1744. She was then cut down to a 50-gun ship and formed part of Anson's fleet at the First Battle of Finisterre in 1747; she was finally broken up in 1769.

I have built two models of her, one at 16'–1" and then a second one at the slightly larger scale of 14'–1" at the express request of my client, who wanted a slightly larger model. Both feature in the photographs.

Lizard 1679

This is another model built to the scale of 16'–1" and was obviously a much simpler project; however in this instance she has been armed and rigged, adding interest to a simpler hull. There is a beautiful Navy Board model of her in the Pitt-Rivers Museum in Oxford.

Syren 1803

Demonstrating the method of framing a model with single and double frames

Although the first section of this book demonstrates techniques used in the framing of a Navy Board model with the characteristically stylised framing that is so unique to their construction, the same basic methods can also be used for more conventionally framed models, the stylised Navy Board framing is only really applicable for models of ships up to about the mid 1740s, after which something closer to full size practice, with either single or double frames, or a combination of both, and with cant frames at bow and stern would be more appropriate.

To illustrate this type of framing I have included photographs of the final two models in this section. The models were built and photographed many years ago with no intention at the time of using them for demonstration purposes, so it is pure chance that I have any pictures taken during the course of their construction. However, I think they illustrate most of the stages of their framing. Any gaps I will endeavour to bridge with the text.

I am going to use the photographs of *Syren*, an American brig built in 1803. The model is to the same scale as *Royal George*, namely 16'–1", as a demonstration model, and I will run through them in the same sequential order as is employed in the main body of the book.

The first difference of note is that because *Syren* is a flush-decked vessel the framed section of the model extends all the way up to the main rail, in fact all the blanks from which the frames will be cut are the height of the model, from the bottom of the frames to their highest point at bow or stern, whichever is the greater. All the square frames are then assembled in a rectangular block. The blanks that are to form double frames can be permanently glued to one another and spacers of suitable thickness veneer glued between the frames with a few blobs of Seccotine in exactly the same manner as was shown for *Royal George*. When the block has finally been assembled, the Seccotine is reinforced by running a little Superglue along the edges of the block to join the extreme corners of the blanks one to another, this is to give more strength and stability to the block ready for the next stage of the work. The block is now run through the table saw to just skim the four sides

1. The whole block now needs to have a groove cut along the length of the top to receive the batten of wood that will locate the model to its building jig and another one along the bottom of the block for the keel. I carry out this work by running it several times over the appropriately lowered blade of the Preac saw. After checking that the block is a comfortable fit to the building jig it can be broken apart into sections at the position of the station lines and each section marked using templates prepared from the plans. They cant then be roughly cut to size and reassembled. Next the cant frames are fitted; this is achieved with the model on the jig, each frame being formed in the following way. A blank, identical to those originally used for the frames is run over the Preac saw making a cut centrally from top

to bottom but not quite all the way through, also a slot is cut on one side to fit the batten (see *Royal George* 4). Now spacers are seccotined to the edges of the frame only, a little Superglue run into the central saw cut and the blank fitted onto the locating batten and held firmly in place against both the jig and model, so closing the saw cut and setting either side at the correct angle; it is held in place until the glue has set. The photograph shows the sections from which the square, cant and frames, along with a solid block from which the extreme stern of the model will be carved, glued together ready for final shaping. (See *Royal George* 10–19)

2. The model after the shaping. Note the line drawn along the broadside delineating the lower edge of the planking, the groove for the keel and the groove I have cut to accept the deadwood. This latter was marked in and carefully cut with knife and file; I have no easy options for this one.

3. After numbering each section (see *Royal George* 22), the model is split apart as shown here and the spacers discarded.

4. The sections disassembled and laid out in sequence.

5. The centres of the frames were then removed with a fretsaw before starting to reassemble the model much along the lines of *Royal George*. New spacers were carefully cut from veneer and fitted between the frames, but only above the line marking the lower edge of the planking. After each frame was added the strip of timber that can be seen in the picture, the same width as the keel, was returned to the model ensuring perfectly aligned reassembly.

6. The reassembly process nearing completion.

7. As with *Royal George* when the framed hull has been completely reassembled, the false top can be removed and the topsides cleaned up. The stern deadwood was cut from a single piece of box and the stem, sternpost, keel and hull planking fitted.

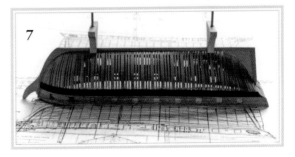

8. The deck beams being installed.

9. A view of the completed deck from above. A small vessel of this vintage would of course have a simpler deck framing arrangement than a large man of war and would make an ideal choice for a first framed miniature.

10. The bow of *Syren*, giving a good view of the forward end of deck with its fittings. I have covered the construction of ships boats, anchors, cannons and carronades and all the other deck paraphernalia built to this scale in my previous book *Period Ship*

Model Making; this could certainly be used in tandem with this volume

As a guide to building a framed flush-decked vessel from, say, the late seventeenth to the mid nineteenth century.

11. Some of the guns before fitting.

12. The stern and aftmost section of the model.

13. The completed model mounted on its plinth.

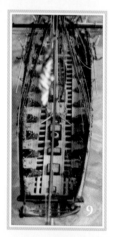

Speedwell 1752

This is a little ship that would be an excellent choice for a model. As a subject it has been well covered elsewhere; there is a series of six articles in *Model Shipwright* Nos 3 to 8 titled *An English Ketch Rigged Sloop* by W H Shoulder, covering the Speedwell Class, and another short article in *Model Shipwright* No. 30 by Dana McCalip. Both of these contain plans of her and a set may also be obtained from the National Maritime Museum, which also holds two contemporary models of ships of the class. The construction of the model follows very closely that of *Syren*.

Lines & Body Plans

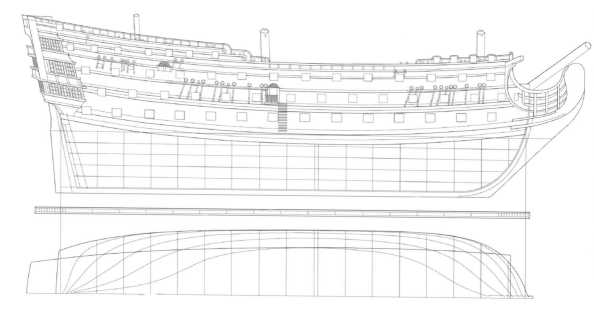

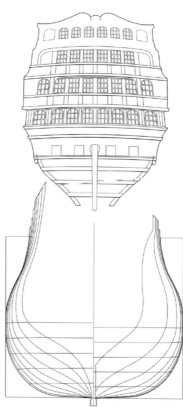

Lines and body plans and profile of *Royal George*. (Drawn by Norman Swales)

⁓ Deck Plans ⁓

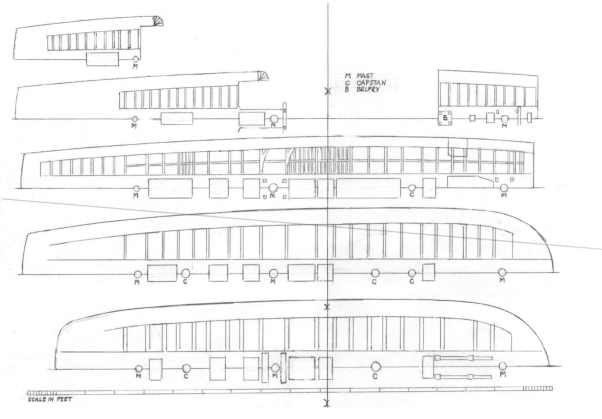

M MAST
C CAPSTAN
B BELFRY

SCALE IN FEET

Deck plans drawn by the author of *Royal George*

⁓ Research Sources ⁓

The following prototypes and drawings will prove invaluable for anyone wishing to build this model.

The plans and profile of the *Royal George*. Drawn by Norman Swales from the original draughts held at the National Maritime Museum Greenwich.

Royal George model, rigged, in the Museum of Fine Arts, Boston, Massachusetts, USA.

Drawing of the *Royal George*, from a series by Thomas Baston, 1721, and engraved by John Cole.

Royal William model in the National Maritime Museum. Cat No SLR0409

Royal William model, rigged, in the National Maritime Museum. Cat No SLR0408

Royal William model, rigged, in the US Naval Academy, Annapolis

Further Reading

Below is a list of books and catalogues which I have found to be useful sources of information during the construction of this and many other models.

Anderson, R C, *Seventeenth-Century Rigging* (London 1955)

Chapelle, Howard Irving, *The History of American Sailing Ships* (New York 1982)
————, *The History of the American Sailing Navy* (New York 1949)

Franklin, John, *Navy Board Ship Models 1650-1750* (London 1989)

Harland, John & Myers, Mark, *Seamanship in the Age of Sail* (London 1984)

Lavery, Brian *The Arming and Fitting of English Ships of War 1600-1815* (London 1987)

Lees, James, *The Masting and Rigging of English Ships of War 1625 – 1860* (London 1979)

Marquardt, Karl Heinz, *Eighteenth-Century Rigs and Rigging* (London 1992)
————, *The Global Schooner* (London 2003)

May W E, *The Boats of Men-of-War* (London 1999)

McLanathan, Richard B K, *Ship Models* (Boston 1957)

McNarry, Donald, *Shipbuilding in Miniature* (London 1982)
————, *Ship Models in Miniature* (London 1975)

Petrejus, E W, *Modelling the Brig of War Irene* (Hengelow 1970)

Stephens, Simon, *Ship Models in the Thompson Collection*, (London 2009)